D1338476

County Council

Libraries, books and more . . .

WITHDRAWN

Please return/renew this item by the last due date.
Library items may be renewed by phone on
030 33 33 1234 (24 hours) or via our website
www.cumbria.gov.uk/libraries

Cumbria Libraries
CLIC
Interactive Catalogue

Ask for a CLIC password

CARLISLE
CA3 8NX

WITH THE
BRITISH ARMY
ON THE SOMME

MEMOIRS FROM THE TRENCHES

BY
SIR WILLIAM BEACH THOMAS

Pen & Sword
MILITARY

This edition published in 2014 by

Pen & Sword Military
An imprint of
Pen & Sword Books Ltd
47 Church Street
Barnsley
South Yorkshire
S70 2AS

This book was first published as 'With the British On the Somme'
by Methuen & Co. Ltd., London, 1917.

ISBN: 9781783463107

A CIP catalogue record for this book is available from the British Library

Printed and bound in England
By CPI Group (UK) Ltd, Croydon, CR0 4YY

Pen & Sword Books Ltd incorporates the imprints of Pen & Sword Aviation, Pen & Sword
Family History, Pen & Sword Maritime, Pen & Sword Military, Pen & Sword Discovery, Pen
& Sword Politics, Pen & Sword Atlas, Pen & Sword Archaeology, Wharncliffe Local History,
Wharncliffe True Crime, Wharncliffe Transport, Pen & Sword Select, Pen & Sword Military
Classics, Leo Cooper, The Praetorian Press, Claymore Press, Remember When, Seaforth
Publishing and Frontline Publishing

For a complete list of Pen & Sword titles please contact

PEN & SWORD BOOKS LIMITED
47 Church Street, Barnsley, South Yorkshire, S70 2AS, England
E-mail: enquiries@pen-and-sword.co.uk
Website: www.pen-and-sword.co.uk

CONTENTS

PART I

PART II

PART I

CHAPTER I
BEFORE THE WAR

I N THE SUMMER of 1912 an English socialist of some fame in the world of letters was returning home through France. On the train he made acquaintance with a highly educated German of a social type scarcely known in England. The man was a merchant, an imperial politician, a commercial traveller of the higher sort, and in some measure a spy - a spy of character and tendencies, a political psychologist who took back to Germany information of the trend of other people's ways and habits. His constant pleasure was to discuss national traits and world politics. With the cold and cruel logic that mark one side of the Prussian character, he proceeded to sketch for the edification of his English companion the course of the impending war.

And he spoke by the book. His prognostics were verified to the letter in many details. He was wrong only as to issues. He told how the German army would pour across Belgium and swamp France. Nor did he omit to give practical details of the material preparations. Wooden platforms, so he said, had been manufactured in sections for the purpose of lengthening the little platforms at particular local stations in Belgium.

The tale would have been very distasteful to his companion, who was what we call a pacifist, if he had not regarded the whole discussion as a mere academic thesis; and in that temper he joined issue. "What will Britain be doing all this while?" He asked. At the challenge the German, who was on his way to accept the hospitality of an aristocratic house in England, unfolded his belief in the utter decadence of Britain, illustrating his theme with examples from the home of his host. Such young men, said the German, are of no use to their country; and the nation that encourages them to shoot and hunt and play games and to drive motors is too selfish and too lazy to fight.

Three years later, after the first harvest of war had been reaped, I went to seek the grave of one of these young Englishmen. He had sought a commission before the war was a week old and joined one of the best of all our fighting regiments. Before many weeks were over he was recognized even in that company as a soldier of exceptional parts. He had made himself expert in the machine-gun and in bombing. Throughout the most desperate and miserable period of the fighting in the mud of Flanders he was never anything but merry and keen. He was one of the few men that ever I knew who enjoyed the war and the exercise of his vitality in such a field. Whatever he may have felt, for he was kind and affectionate by nature and a great lover of children, he never showed to his companions a sign of fear or reluctance or softness. "Whom the gods love die young." He was shot dead in the defence of a German trench that his company had captured against heavy odds. Where he fell, there he was buried, far from the many acres he would one day have owned. He was rich and strong and comely; and made the supreme sacrifice. The nation that is decadent in his fashion may gladly embrace the German accusation. It was no accident that he wrested this wretched trench from a stronger force of the apostles of the art of war. The formula, baldly stated again and again in German histories, "We are the greatest people because we are the most warlike," went by the board once again during that fight for the muddy ditch in Flanders. The better man won.

One other anecdote. Three weeks before the war an English trades unionist and internationalist went to Hamburg for a conference convoked to discuss internationalism and the solidarity of labour. The Englishman had previously persuaded the Hamburg workmen to organize co-operative shops, and they began to prove successful beyond all German expectation. Presently the military authorities descended, visited the organizers, took a complete census of horses and carts, offering a small retaining fee. At the same time these officers made a record of every machine in the district and instructed the owners in the best and quickest method of converting the machinery to the manufacture of war material.

All this was known to the trades unionists of Germany.

Because of this knowledge, or in spite of it, no single deputy of the German socialist group present at the conference could be persuaded to vote for a motion in favour of international peace, though the discussion was purely abstract and academic. The pacifists themselves believed that the world could not compete with Krupp and the lesser Krupps in war as in peace, and had definitely, if not always consciously, accepted the policy of an aggressive war. They felt no doubt that a quick and thorough victory would follow and would ensue the paradise of world dominance. The prospect was too fair to reject. Even the best succumbed to the enticement of the dream. When August came the socialists in the Reichstag cheered the Chancellor to the echo.

All the world that loved peace could do nothing else but fight a people of such a mood and temper.

CHAPTER II
THE SOLDIER AND THE SEËR

EVERY ONE WHO, not being a soldier, writes about war, sees more of its pomp and circumstance than its dirt and stagnancy. If anyone were to write of it as it is at its worst - as it was in the mine holes at St. Eloi, where strong men fell exhausted within a hundred yards from their starting-point - as it was in Devil's Wood, where bodies lay thick - as it was in the crowded trenches down the hill towards Le Sars, where more men were buried alive than shot dead, then man and woman would not endure to read the tale, if anyone could endure to write it or consent to publish it. Nothing is written, even in Zola's *Débâcle*, as unendurable as half that our men suffered up to the second battle of Ypres and after. Perhaps the worst ought to be told to the end that, on the way to the "far-off divine event," men may be finally sickened of war and feel its bestiality in their veins for the rest of their lives.

Yet only a few men could so write it, and they must come from the ranks of those who have themselves known the worst. If written as an imparted tale, it would be no more than morbid, unwholesome, false.

In the following account of what I have seen and experienced during the later part of the war, I do not propose to attempt to tell an unpleasant tale, to underline horrors, to double dye hospital scenes, to accent failures and impress death and wounds. But it is the duty of every reader of a war book to feel as he reads that war is war, that every "glorious" victory or "magnificent" resistance or "masterly" retreat means the extinction of life and a sum of pain beyond computation. Nothing imaginable is worse than the atmosphere of trench warfare. Men crouch in mud and are pashed out of existence by bits of metal thrown from miles away. The chemicals that explode destroy the hearing, displace the heart, set the nerves in a quiver which may last lifelong. To pain is added madness, to wounds suffocation. Even when men charge in the open and taste for a moment the ecstasy of struggle, they are usually so weary from want of sleep that life is already a burden, and as soon as the victory is won, the crouching in the mud begins again, and often hunger and thirst are added. Modern war is of this nature. Every man hates it, save one in ten thousand whose "faculty for storm and turbulence" is beyond the normal, or whose passion against the enemy is supreme.

Yet war is wonderful as well as gross, majestic as well as muddy. That full sentence of Napier's, "With what a majesty the British soldier fights," goes ringing in the head even when a knock-kneed soldier from the slums falls gasping in the mud at the bottom of a crazy ditch. Humour and good humour laugh on the parapet of death, and health sprouts from the centres of mud and reek. Ideals of faith and loyalty shine through the curses and blasphemy that often pour from the mouth of the fighter. Even the most insensate soldier will religiously exclude from his letters home anything that might breathe alarm or hint danger. What war is morally, it is also aesthetically. Its grandeur - to the eyes, though never to the mind - may be overwhelming. It may even be pretty or, as soldiers say, "amusing." Its contrasts cover the field of contrasts. But, the nearer, the uglier, is the rule; and soldiers have nothing more irritating to endure than the pictures of battles as they seem to distant observers. I write with one special contrast in mind. One evening I had the news that just before dawn our troops were to attack an intrusive angle of German trench at St. Eloi. The only chance of seeing anything of the fight was to climb one of those mounds, rather than hills, which some mole-like upheaval has raised on the plains of Flanders. All that I saw during this night and morning was of surpassing charm. A sensitive woman would have enjoyed every moment. Nature and art were combined to invest the spectacle with splendour. The sun rose blood-red. The shrapnel hung like clouds painted by old masters to hold mediaeval angels. The horizon glittered with firefly sparks. In spite of the tumult the first songs of spring . were twittered in the hedgerow. Good news reached us. All was well with the world.

Such the semblance. What the reality? The soft and sticky ground at St. Eloi had been tossed up as loosely as hay behind the tedders by one mine after another. The sloping sides of the great hollows were further fretted with shells and bombs, till the earth was crumbled out of all consistency. Rain had fallen and reduced the carious particles to a state of foul swampiness, to a Slough of Despond, where men waded to the hips and only the strongest could cross. In this cockpit the Royal Scots and others charged and struggled. They saw their wounded sink out of sight. A friend, struggling to rescue a friend, sank himself, and the two looked across at one another, each helpless. For a day and a night and a day under the rain of heathenish shells and grenades our men wrestled to turn these pits into fortresses and keep back the enemy from a few paltry yards of Flanders. Not once or twice men have been drowned from sheer weariness in the water of the trenches. These men were drowned in mud. In primeval slime they fought like lions a battle of eels, and in the sequel when they had done their utmost certain topographical features made the place unwise to hold. I spoke with the men who had endured this the day after writing of the battle as it was unveiled to me, and felt that I had committed unconscious high treason. So easy is it to make the foul appear fair, to be tricked by the enchantment of distance.

Perhaps the general attitude of every soldier to everything written about war - and not least the official news - is that all is too smooth, too pretty, too little real, and too favourable. It is true what some have endured to suffer others must endure to hear; but readers must submit to be tricked. Avoidance of the brutality of war is in some sort inevitable. All who have written about war, especially the great historians, who are doubly deceived by the distance of time and space, see it as the airman sees it in a large spaciousness where details are hid and only issues count. But let us remember the real war behind. If we forget the loss, the pain, the fear, the waste, and the wickedness, we forget a duty to the human race.

Again, the thousands who have publicly praised the man in the trench, whether soldier or officer, have unwittingly in their cumulative admiration helped to give - or so the soldier sometimes thinks - a wrong impression of his service.

The truth is that the observer is so constantly struck by the cheerfulness of the men that he has come to regard their occupation as in itself an almost cheerful thing, or rather to give the impression that it is a cheerful thing. Every visitor to the front has so far escaped without hurt; and most visitors have seen few tragic and many singularly picturesque sights. Even in the trenches goodly cooking smells titillate his nostrils; and if the day is quiet and rifle grenades are infrequent, he is conscious, as he reaches the fighting line, of a curious feeling of security after the tremors of his approach.

Afterwards, when he returns home, he is apt to give a picture of the war which leaves the soldiers a little resentful. Somehow the trimmings and dressings come to smother up the reality, and the fact does not appear that life in the trenches is no soft, pretty, or sentimental thing. Let me add yet another illustration of the soldier's point of view in face of his admirers.

On the morrow of a severe local attack I went to visit the neighbourhood of the scene of action close to the famous Hohenzollern Redoubt. No picture could have been more idyllic. There was great aerial activity. The machines looked like silvered butterflies chasing one another on a summer morning. Even the sound of the machine guns, followed by the patter of the bullets here and there, was dwarfed by the great space of intervening air to the tap of a nesting woodpecker. Even when a plane was hit - and I saw one hit - it slid to earth like a homing seabird, giving no sense of catastrophe. The shrapnel made soft pillows for a cupid's bust. The general scene, viewed from a point of vantage, had the glamour that sunshine following snow can give to any landscape, even after it has suffered such earthquake shocks as disfigured part of the land in front of me.

Nearer the front some of the dug-outs were comfortable and home-like. In one the only complaint was that the lire was rather big. Its occupant was reading a list of names of men recommended for gallant action. Farther back at a headquarters every one was exceedingly elated at the results of the fighting: the science of the engineers, the quick charge, the few casualties. The journey to and from the front could scarcely have been more charming. My companion, who was new to these things, was especially pleased with the parties of men swinging along with towels round their shoulders, as if they were at a seaside resort. This was on the return journey. Earlier the birds had heralded a delicious dawn with a fresh and lively chorus. In very truth, all was well with the world. My companion and I had spent a morning sweet with news of victory and the benediction of the spring. Who said WAR?

That is one picture. Now for the other. On the night following an old and grizzled officer, almost the last of those who had marched with the regiment to Mons and back two years ago, received instructions to take his men up to hold the ground won. The landscape he surveyed before moving was a model of desolation, ugly with debris and foul confusion, showing up against an ominous mountain of slag, converted to a German fortress, a monument of "clinkered sin." As he and his men felt their way forward they met the stretcher-bearers and their groaning burdens.

The first crater they reached was a valley of Gehenna strewed with bodies, all fouled with mud so deep that only the strongest could attempt to carry out the wounded, and even the fresh and unimpeded troops had much ado to advance. At last they took up their stations in this same bottomless mud and slush, some of them over ground beneath which they knew the enemy were tunnelling, all of them in positions open to every danger from above. Each man had only one course - to shut his mind to any thought whatever, beyond an almost fatalistic determination to hold on, to carry on, to go through with it. And they held on. They made good, splendidly, grimly. But the splendour was not pretty, not of a sort to make the men enjoy delicate appreciations of the amenities of trench life.

The very worst side of war can never be given while war lasts; and for this reason the soldier thinks that people at home, while they praise his cheerful courage, do not understand how grim his business is. The lighter side of war is daily painted; the darker side seldom and less adequately.

Of course, the journeyman work of the war, in the front trench or behind it, is at neither extreme; and as time went on it improved for all our troops in all parts of the line. Our artillery became more numerous than the enemy's and fired many times more shells. The trench maladies were more or less defeated. Confidence grew. Some few men even enjoyed war.

All this is true; but injustice is done and a false view promulgated if the civilian world does not realize that every little success won, every little attack defeated, means a very terrible experience to every man engaged. In the greatest battles in history few episodes have more finely tested our British sort of courage or better revealed the grimness of war than the battles on the Somme, for local defeats and the snare of muddy stagnancy were associated with salient victory. And yet at the very time when the worst was in progress the edge of the battle disclosed scenes so picturesque - I might almost say so pretty - as almost to make a visitor oblivious of the gaunt, utter ruin of the once happy towns through which he passed or where he stood.

CHAPTER III
STEPS TO THE SOMME: MOVEMENT

T HE BATTLE OF the Somme, opened at 7.30 on the morning of 1st July, cut the year in half by a single blow. It dissevered all the past from the present, so complete was the change of warfare, in spirit and in fact. The battles were fought in a fair country of hill and valley, and men moved for a great part of the while in the open, instead of crouching in muddy ditches on a viewless plain. We had fled and forgotten for a while

"the ditches
And tunnels of Poverty Flat."

The issues became vast and positive. They had been meagre and static. Above all, we heard every day such cluttering of shells that the very whine and whinny overhead drowned other noises.

But the battle of the Somme was the result of growth, the flower of a biennial plant. Just before it opened, as I was watching our shells playing pitch and toss with German wire opposite the Gommecourt salient, I began discussing in the narrow prison of an observation post the years that had led to this event. The artillery observer said almost bitterly that now people would forget the early war and the first soldiers. For myself, though I had been in France from September 1914, I was to see this battle as I had never seen war; but vivid moments survive from the first two years, and the tale of the Somme will be truer and more real for some glimpses into earlier fights.

The war began with movement, at one time almost the quickest known in war; and such is the influence of movement, that even amid the nameless confusion of the retreat from Mons, when men, if they slept at all, only slept as they moved, officers confessed that they enjoyed every moment. The enjoyment was doubled when the battle of the Marne was won, and our army marched north again; and every one believed himself engaged in a short, sharp war, already reaching a climax.

One officer, who still asserts that he never really knew the delight of life till the days of the retreat, nor so hated it as in the stagnant days that followed our advance, touched every variety of experience in that August and September. He heard the French cheers coming faintly over the water at Havre, when the news was made sure that the English were coming. With a hundred French civilians he dug in a nightmare night those shallow trenches at Le Cateau, which were afterwards described as our "prepared position" He rode with a staff north and south, arresting here and there German military spies, one careering in all the glory of a 60-h.p. Mercédès car. He stood for hours by the roadside among the mingled succession of guns, cavalry, companies or platoons of infantry, Red Cross cars, ordnance lorries, and the rest, helping to sort out the British Army. Experience fell so quick on experience that not a moment was left to think of the bearing of it all. Action filled every moment. The army was sorted between Hem and Noyon. The men slept, and divisions recovered cohesion. The Marne was fought and won; and a fortnight later this officer, still riding the same horse - an animal well known in the Grafton hunt - found himself journeying north a few miles east of his retreat to the south. With him were two other officers, and close behind six mounted orderlies, each leading an extra mount. Suddenly one of the party caught sight of a head-dress of curious appearance topping a stook of corn in an adjacent field. "Germans, by the Prophet," he cried, and the whole party jumped the little ditch at the roadside and trotted up the stubble. From the vast hand of the leading officer stuck out by an inch or two the muzzle of a little pistol, and as they rode the others chaffed him on his absurd toy. The orderlies loaded their rifles, but as the led steeds pulled them this way and that, they were like to be more dangerous to friends than enemies, and one of the party begged them most earnestly to put their rifles away.

Happily the Germans were not in fighting mood. The gentleman playing hide-and-seek behind the stook gracefully surrendered, and soon called up his friends, to the number of 120 odd, who were in hiding in the wood. A little later than the day of this incident I found myself at the village alongside the wood where the men had hidden. They were the relics of a tough rear guard action, one of the very first won by aerial observation; and I saw a picture which was not to be repeated till the days of the battle of the Somme.

The hope of victory, the sense of pursuit, bred of the German retreat, were to live in suspended animation for nearly two years. The German had won great victories, had suffered a great defeat. He was to fight at Ypres two drawn battles against meagre lines of troops starved of ammunition. By what incompetence and lack of dash he failed to win we cannot yet tell. But it is certain that if the German leaders had been half as good as they claim to be, they would have broken our line and marched almost where they would.

Walking farther north, as I approached the Aisne I met a British soldier returning to his regiment after escaping from German hands; and a wonderful story he had to tell: how the prisoners, who were retained under shell-fire to dig trenches, lay down for the night in one long line, with a sentry at either end. After one more than usually laborious day, men and sentries were so dog tired that all slept deeply, except my friend. He slipped from the line, first making a dummy figure of himself on the ground. He crawled to the sentry, robbed him of some papers, slipped into a neighbouring wood, lay hidden for twenty-four hours, then set out - vaguely, in any direction. He was grazed by a bullet over the eye as he swam a river; he "borrowed" an old horse and rode some miles; he fed on corn and berries, but at last crossed north of the rival lines and wandered down into the area of British troops, where finally he found his unit.

As I listened to his tale over a game of cribbage in a little inn, a gunner sergeant came in and asked me the way to Villers-Cotteret. He was TO START FOR BELGIUM at five the next morning. The last violent German attacks against our lines on the Aisne had failed.

The battle of the Aisne, where the British Army fought an heroic fight almost unchronicled, was over. The race for the sea was beginning. I was off before the sergeant, and, by walking twenty-five miles as fast as might be, reached Paris early in the afternoon. Seventeen hours in the train took me to Calais, and four more to Hazebrouck. From the neighbourhood of St. Omer we saw two Uhlans across the fields, and the excitement was great. People were differently affected. Two French soldiers, who had sick leave, at once took out their knives and ripped the stripes over their tunics. It was said, they explained, that the Germans were much more severe towards any captive who carried distinctions, and the simple *poilu* had a better time than his N.C.O.

The train was the train for Lille, according to the shouted information of the porter at Calais. After much nervous vacillation, during which guards, stationmasters, and drivers consulted with passengers, who included a most worthy and courageous deputy, it was decided to go as far as Hazebrouck. The Uhlans had reached it first, forty of them, but had gone again, leaving dead two railway officials and a little girl. In the afternoon, from among a bunch of French dragoons ambushed in the thistles beside the railway, I watched a sharp and yet nearly bloodless action. A battery of 75's, a few machine-gunners, and several squadron of horse routed the enemy's patrols for the day.

Next morning the town was evacuated. No one knew where anyone was; and as I set out to walk again I met little groups of dragoons, looking strangely mediaeval as they emerged from the autumn mists; and each group asked me in turn whether I had happened to notice any Germans about or heard of their doings. Behind them came the British, also feeling their way forward and pushing the enemy back. A month later sketchy holes, dug in rough order, dotted the line of trenches that the rival armies still hold. A friend of mine, afterwards to become a general, was guided to one such hole the evening of his arrival. He had the vaguest sense of the places where his neighbours were. All that he felt quite sure of was that an officer had been killed in his hole the day before. The thought kept him wakeful. As the dawn approached he could see frozen on the edge of the pit the brains of his predecessor.

A moment later horror was absorbed in expectancy. Dim through the thin wood he saw a figure approaching, very slowly, very cautiously, and the green uniform blended well with the mist and dying leaves. A vagrant German sharpshooter was afoot, turning his head this way and that as he advanced with extreme caution, and he did not divert his attention for a second until, at a point within 40 yards, a fallen tree blocked his path. Then for a moment he looked down to surmount the obstacle, and in that moment lost his life. The sniper was sniped, the Englishman avenged. The German's musket clattered from his hand, and his body fell prone over the tree. This British officer had seen and killed a German at his first venture. Thereafter, when those holes developed into complicated trenches, soldiers were to live in them for a year, for two years perhaps - to live in them and maybe to die in them without ever seeing an enemy and seldom firing a rifle.

In those days it was held a crime to wish to chronicle any event in which the British Army was engaged. So, like many others, I came to know much of the battle of the Yser, little of the battle of Ypres. Indeed, for a while all Britain, all the world that read newspapers, felt that the greater brunt was once again borne by Belgium. The struggles at Ypres, and indeed at Arras, were fought *in camera*. Both Belgian and British were begging help of the French, who were themselves harried at many points and in fear of being broken at one. But it is true that the Germans were thrusting for Calais in lieu of Paris, and the Belgians stopped the hole. I saw their wounded - 8000 of them and more - struggle back on the road to Calais, and presently visited day after day the scene of their strange victory.

It was won in part by a civilian, a Justice of the Peace who lived in the charming square of Furnes. He had found in an historical manuscript, which he showed me, an account of the flooding of the lowlands in the opening of the eighteenth century. He submitted the passage to the military authorities, and they took the hint. The sluices were broken and the Germans swept off their legs by the flood. Trenches were dug by the Belgians just on the hither side, fronting the most miserable prospect man could desire. Behind them were the flattened houses and crazy towers of such villages as Ramscapelle and Pervyse. In front the floods dandled the dead bodies of Germans, who moved grotesquely as the waters rose; swelled out to inordinate proportions the bodies of cows fixed upright by the legs in the soft mud; lapped with the sucking noise of a gobbling monster the very head of the parapet. But the floods had done their work. The last German offensive on the West was over for the season.

The muddy brutality of war soaked into the bones of every man, though soldiers were amazingly cheerful. On the Christmas Eve of 1914 I spent an almost merry day in the trenches of Ramscapelle, one of the several shattered villages facing this melancholy inundation; and on Christmas morning journeyed home with a long-legged British officer caked in mud to the hips. By brilliant moonlight he had crept from his trench in front of Ypres - communication trenches there were none - found a chance lorry, which took him to St. Omer, and there he just caught a train that brought him to the Calais boat. He reached his Gloucestershire home in time to dress for Christmas dinner, as merry as a boy at the prospect.

CHAPTER IV
STEPS TO THE SOMME: STAGNATION

THE GERMAN DOMINANCE at Ypres had not affected the spirit of our troops. Some evidence there is that the Germans, having failed to push an overwhelming advantage in men and material, were the more depressed. They thought more seriously of peace at the end of 1914 than ever again till Christmas 1916. Would any of us, soldier or civilian, have kept a cheerful spirit if we could then have envisaged 1915? I picture the first half of it as a hospital, through which percolates an unceasing stream of wounded soldiers, moaning of the enemy's artillery. "Our guns never shoot. We never hear them. The enemy is firing all day and all night." The moan rose unceasingly till even the nurses, who seldom ask of the patients a word about the war, went about begging officers to tell them what this might mean.

And none could answer. The war appeared to consist of Ypres and nothing but Ypres. Our army had the sense of being overlooked - almost in both senses of the word. The German kite balloons went up when and where they wished. Every one who moved up or back had the feeling that an evil eye was upon him. The artillery suffered even more. One young and promising gunner was so oppressed by the eyes of one of these balloons watching every flash of his guns that he could control no longer the insensate desire to strike back, and turned one of his field-guns to an aerial tilt against it. Instantly, of course, the German observer telephoned to his battery, and they smothered our battery with 5.9 shells. Another vainly begged leave to run a single gun forward for the relief of firing a dozen rounds at this "unsleeping Eremite." The running up of the balloons was everywhere signal for trouble. For example, a gunner noticed two rise at a wide angle, and said at once to his companion:

"Let us wait and see what they are going to strafe." Within ten minutes two shells fell on either side of a church. The third hit it, and for a few minutes the two watched "as pretty a piece of gunnery as you could wish." It finished with four incendiary shells, which set the ruins ablaze. Then when the storm seemed over they went to look close at the effect. In front of them walked an old Frenchman and his wife, who owned a house just beside the church. The old man hurried forward, and in a minute came out with a jar under his arm containing 120 golden louis d'or. The old couple smiled, almost fondled the jar, and tottered off down the street.

> *"But ever at my back I hear*
> *Time's winged chariot hurrying near."*

A thin note sang behind them: another shell was on its way. It pitched in the street close beside them, broke the old people into pieces, and scattered the golden pieces all over the street. There was like to be a scramble for the gold even at that time and place, when the gunner intervened and sent off the collected pieces to the Assistant Provost Marshal for due distribution to next of kin.

We suffered from such overlooking by the evil eyes of the enemy all the year in most places, at any rate from Ypres to Arras. All the while destruction accumulated. I was in Arras in November 1914, the day after the Germans had put 500 shells into the old Town Hall. At several different dates in the next eighteen months I repeated the visit. Each time the ruin of the cathedral and the squares and the station was greater. Each time other streets had tumbled in. A few valiant women still sold cards and souvenirs in the square, and slept in the immense cellars; but desolation triumphed. You felt as if you had come to a world where an evil principle ruled and would always rule, increasing gloom and accumulating wretchedness. The devil would never die. Every day he destroyed beauty. Every day he killed life. Extinction seemed the only end.

Such mood was upon us all during 1915. In the spring we were overwhelmed by gas and guns at Ypres. In the autumn the victory of Loos dwindled to a half-defeat. The armies faced one another in stagnant, immobile, sulky wretchedness. "When will the war end?" Said a German officer as he travelled in a hospital train for Boulogne. "I can't tell you when it will end; but I can tell you where - exactly on the spot where we now crouch."

Both sides began to feel this stale hopelessness; but never were soldiers more admirable than ours. They bore every ill. Their positions were worse than the enemy's - their trenches wetter and at first their equipment inferior. But they kept their calmness and their good temper and their will to win. The trenches round Kemmel and Armentières - which were especially familiar to me - were more cheerful places at Christmas 1915 than the Ramscapelle trenches in 1914. The army was growing, and the mingling of troops from many quarters of the world gave a certain impetus. I always found that a visit to the front trench gave a sense of ready cheerfulness, in spite of the mud and nearness to the enemy. One visit to the Canadians, whose lines ran within 40 yards of the Germans, remains very vivid, and will give an epitome of the life. It was a day of mist and rain; and the horizon shrank from ten miles to one as we journeyed to the trenches in the plain, where a horizon from 20 to 30 yards is all that a man needs. Indeed, down in "the common crofts" certain advantages belong to thick weather.

Where the communication trench is a slough you may clamber on to the bank and try to feel as confident as your guide that the enemy will neither see you nor infer you. You take short cuts here and there, trusting that the member of the working party is quite accurate when he assures you that the interval is "dead ground for bullets," though the idiom has an uncomely sound.

A comforting though rather ominous silence was over everything that day; and when we reached the front-line trench the crack of a sniper's rifle just round the traverse sounded as loud as a battery.

But the trenches themselves gave every confidence. Neat drains from No Man's Land flowed out under the duck-boarding that everywhere served as flooring. Even the slither of this stone less mud clay had been kept tame by wire and wood; and the millions of sandbags were piled in the newest and most scientific manner.

As I stopped leaning up against "the loaferburnished wall," while some one else was peering through a spy-hole, I became aware of a sort of rabbit-hole below me. The inmate, with the usual quick Canadian hospitality, offered me the freedom of his dwelling. He could not receive the whole of his guest: there was not room for that. I considered the invitation as extending to my head, and that could enter far enough to see and appreciate the whole of the Dutch interior. The owner sat low before a tiny stove, and he held in his hand a well lathered shaving brush. His cheeriness, conspicuous even in this cheery group, was due perhaps to the prospect of a clean shave, as the preface to a savoury lunch, whose fumes already made a pleasant accompaniment to the toilet.

It is difficult at such a moment to understand and feel the hardship and danger of this daily warfare. The men make you forget it, so natural and jolly they are, though each is in some sense treading on a mine. Every one looks at home. From the next dugout came the gay whistle of "Susanne, Susanne, we love you to a man." On the back wall at the traverse beyond was a little hand-made weathercock, such as you see in a village garden at home. Who would ever have thought that it was put up to indicate the winds favourable to a Hun gas attack?

The gongs fixed to the walls here and there have a domestic look, though they are made of empty shell cases. But most of all the household ways of the men and their lively spirit kept aloof the sense of danger and death. Yet these never for a minute lack a reminder.

Lying on a mud heap were two French rifles dug up yesterday, relics of a stubborn fight on this same spot a year before. The place is fathom-deep in the crudest form of war record. Here and there, in the area of the trench and at its edges, rough circles and crosses mark the burial-spot of the often nameless dead. And you may see more direct evidence than this. Nor can the most buoyant talk quite avoid the tale of losses and scenes still printed on the mind and distinct on the retina. In spite of all, no one is less morbid than the man who fights daily. He thinks first and last of his job; and great thinkers have reached no sounder philosophy or source of comfort.

The day was remaining quiet as well as thick. The mist, now turned to rain, seemed to have blanketed the animosity of guns and grenades, always excepting the rifle of the sniper. And sniping, the most interesting occupation, is also the favourite theme of trench conversation, as may easily be understood. In this very trench a single sniper had just earned a few days' leave after killing his thirty-first German. They were all down in the notebook as certainties with details.

Many were the tales of the skill of one particular German sniper. His prowess was even shown off to visitors, as if he were a recognized attraction of the locality. "Just you watch him" a man would say, and thereupon raise a tin on a stick. Before the visitor was well aware of what was being done, the tin rattled and flew off the stick to the other side of the trench. "Pretty good, isn't he?" The showman would add, with conscious pride that his pet had come up to promise.

No Man's Land came at that date second on the list of trench subjects, but it had another name in this particular district . A visiting general asked some question about the work of the patrols in No Man's Land, and received an answer as satisfactory as unexpected. "We do not call it No Man's Land any longer," said the subaltern. "It is now christened Canada." He spoke with justifiable pride. The space has been annexed so completely that no German has been known to venture upon it for a month and more.

English county troops in some much worse trenches, continually knocked about by trench mortars and approached by alleys that were often canals, kept their Christmas almost as if at home. Yet every man hated the war and longed for an end of which he got no glimpse. A real advance seemed the least likely event in the wide world. The duty of duties was mere endurance; and it was nobly done, after the established fame of the English. But no men ever had a greater longing for home. The Christmas post proved that.

CHAPTER V
STEPS TO THE SOMME: EXPECTANCY

THE MOOD OF 1915 continued into 1916. For myself I traipsed about front trenches and support trenches and alleys all along the line, week in and week out, seeing nothing but mud and water, and feeling each week that the treadmill of war would never cease, but that round and round the survivors would wheel till human nature could endure no more. The trenches from Gommecourt to Vaux on the Somme looked permanent and immovable as the rest. Who shall say when the real change came, but as the spring of 1916 advanced soldiers began to see and feel that the force of the nation was steadily mounting. France as well as England was becoming a great school of war, where every soldier was being trained for a vital issue at some nearing date. I remember with peculiar distinctness the day when in my own experience the sense of stagnancy gave way to expectancy. I had stayed the night in the fine monastery that crowns the Mont des Cats, a hill that rivals Cassel itself or the Scherpenberg as a vantage-point for the Flanders plain.

From where I stood, watching the battle from afar on a quiet Sunday morning in January, the landscape below, with its patterned fields and pencilled avenues and dotted homesteads, was so wide and sweet that the commotion of war and its equipment, in spite of their insistence, seemed as little and paltry as the bickering of a bevy of sparrows.

This Flemish hill commands so wide a rural view that the line of battle is enclosed and lost within the wide margins, and though these margins themselves, through all their depth, are scribbled over with the unlovely writing of war the country wins. Peace and its elemental arts conquer.

You look at the war with a sort of idle curiosity, as you would at the rooks mobbing a sparrow-hawk down by the hopfield poles. The scene of it is spread out like a painted map. When the mist is blown aside and the sun is out you can see from the Nieuport dunes to La Bassee and the coal tips. Indeed, there are few such wide views in Europe as this and four or five other neighbour hillocks offer. On that Sunday morning all the nearer fields and hop gardens and spinneys were stencilled with the clear precision proper to a winter day; but the war zone lay fitly cloaked under the decent cere-cloth of an even haze. The inclination was to look at near and homely things - the elm tree twigs already in tiny leaf and the open buds of the guelder.

The sunshine was brilliant but variable; and presently the patch of light, clouded on the hilltop, moved away to the valley and toward the battle, carrying our eyes with it. Then, like the sun in Ajalon, it stopped; and the light was concentrated, almost stagily, on one disc in the else misty distance.

To my utter amazement a great ruined town lay suddenly visible- the once quiet, almost cloistral Ypres, with its jumble of formless homes and streets and broken spires. The stump of the Cloth Hall tower with the ugly gap in its side could be picked out before the patch of light moved on and showed Zonnebeke away in the German lines. The scene and the mood in which you watched it were at once turned inside out. You forgot the buds for the battle - a change very much for the worse.

Even in the sunshine you could see the quick stab of flame from some assassinating battery else hidden and unsuspected in some meadow or tilth. This fire seen in a bright light has always a peculiarly venomous look among the signals of war. Many warlike things are themselves almost peaceful. From that distance the puffs of shrapnel behind Ypres had a woolly, comfortable appearance, as if cherubs' heads could rest comfortably in them, after the fashion of a gentle decorative Raphael picture. The slow boom of the heavy guns is itself like the roll of the sea; and there is nothing more harmless in guise than the modern battle line itself.

I once walked up to within 800 yards of the enemy's line on a hill in Flanders without the least sense that in the harmless rustic ditches below me the greatest army in the world was fighting the greatest and the most brutal war of the world. But the flash of flame, that "lightning of the nations," is angry beyond all concealment. There is no mistaking it. It is the very expression of the joy of killing. The serpent in Eden spitting venom.

At such a place on such a day the conflict ion of war and peace is strangely abrupt. The church bell is ringing. Within the monastery, the old monks, pledged to a life of silence, kneel and read and contemplate. The country people, in Sunday dress, dawdle in twos and threes up and along the hill discussing the early signs of spring, or the pleasant warmth of the parish church, or the price of food, or the probable paucity of trippers come Easter.

It would need some force vastly greater than Armageddon to drive out of the heads of any country people their common daily homely thoughts. They are busy with things more important than war; and to minds well regulated by everyday concourse with nature much more interesting and honourable. The presence of war goes for the most part simply unheeded, though it is urgent enough in all conscience. And this hill was an epitome of it.

By the pleasant spinney on the sunny side is a little graveyard where six Indian soldiers are buried. The wooden tomb-heads bear names that are the Smiths of the Indian Empire. One only is marked "Sepoy. Unknown." These fine fellows met their death at this place during a fight in which the notorious Prince Maximilian of Hesse fell. He is buried in a grave kept secret from all but a few.

What prophet in the wildest Cassandra flight of imagination would have dared to foretell that such opponents could ever have met on such a tilting ground? The old round mill on the hill-top has seen six hundred years of warfare, but never such an historical marvel as this. The signs of war are everywhere. The old mill itself is scarred by an

English shell. The monks' wall is pitted by machine gun fire. Cunning German trenches furrow the hill-side, and bits of their thin black telephone wire are coiled in the hedgerow.

The impression might have been as of "old, unhappy, far-off things and battles long ago," had not the Sunday calm been broken by a variety of the noises of war, very near and very real. Rifles cracked, bombs exploded, a mortar fired, aeroplanes boomed loud overhead. Puffs of smoke rose from among the trees. The war at hand, though ten miles from the front, was the noisier, the more various. The truth was that the whole countryside had become a training-ground. Snipers' schools, bombers' schools, trench-mortar schools, infantry schools were dotted about in every other parish. The British nation was at the school of war, preparing for - what? In some schools lines of sacks were hung up for bayonet practice, and they looked like corpses. Flying over the country in a plane, I saw below scores of practice trenches and little squads of men drilling, charging, wire-laying. Day after day along the roads fantastic monsters on caterpillar wheels grunted their slow way forward. No scenes in the war more moved the emotion than the regiments landing at the base night after night on the dark quays and gathering in squares lit by a few dull flares and crunching away in column between lines of French women and children wishing them well. These and a score of sights seen earlier at the base moved like a cinema across the mind's eye. The intention, the will, the momentum of the nation made themselves felt at every turn; and from that date - for me at any rate - the war grew more and more exciting as less and less happened. The waters were mounting inch by inch. The flood must come.

Along the roads ranks of lorries were packed, a hundred in line, and in the fields the grass or field crop was paved for acres with standing for horses. The cavalry held field days. The infantry made sham attacks with all the paraphernalia of smoke and bombs. Mines were blown up to practise the infantry in charging and consolidating, while over their heads the trench mortars sent festoons of shells.

Perhaps even the peasants felt a breath of the excitement, as the thud of the bombs interrupted the prayers of the monks and the laughter of the school children. But the sense was subconscious. For the peasant, noble man that he is, history may stand on its head and civilization explode in powder. It is an early spring nevertheless, and "wonderful mild for the time of year."

All these things were more obvious to a traveller behind the lines than to the men in the trenches, who were busy rather with the present improvement of life than with the possibilities for the future.

Trenches were still canals; and trench life was only saved from gloom by the refusal of men or officers to appear dismal. Never before did gaiety so prove itself a quality of courage. In these months a merry heart went more than all the way, for it made good travelling for a score at a time. Life was hard; but, as the spring advanced, less and less hard. The engineers came to the rescue, and staff officers turned their attention to hygiene. "We are become nursemaids," one said, half in mockery, half in pride.

The Guards had already designed and erected draining works for the trenches that involved many miles of piping. Waterworks were set up miles in the rear. The better regiments had great washhouses and "municipal establishments." Beneficent socialism reigned. All men who came from the trenches bathed in hot water, and after foot inspection, dressed in clean clothes. All deficiencies in equipment were made good. Late, but at last (after great store of goloshes had arrived and been returned!), "gum-boots" of the right size were provided in due quantity; and the malady of trench feet vanished. How constant the threat was, one instance will explain. In the St. Eloi salient, where one troop was forced to hold for three days without full relief, a German shell hit the store of gum boots left by the outgoing battalion. The men were therefore forced to be content with their ordinary boots, as every one was forced in the early days. The result was an immediate crop of cases of "trench foot," the first seen by the doctors in that neighbourhood for several months. Later, trench helmets were provided for every soldier, and they have saved several thousand lives. Railways - though still inadequate - multiplied. Day by day more howitzers struggled along the road and stores of ammunition lumbered up. France behind the line was a great training school, an Aldershot, Divisions, as well as corps and armies, had their fields of instruction. At the bases, where the scale of work began to astound all neutral observers who were allowed to visit them, one saw as great an effort in state socialism as the world has known. Every man in the employ of the army was provided with good food, good boots, good clothing. His old things were mended and, better, returned to him. He was not allowed to go ill clad or fed or to do harm to his health; and, after excesses of extravagance in the early days, meticulous care was taken to retrieve and salve all the worn and jettisoned material: guns, bicycles, saddles, ammunition cases, tags of leather, and the rest.

The sense for right action in war grew in every direction, in the domain of "Intelligence" as well as "Operations," to use the two words which divide the War Office. Instead of alternate promises and harryings, an official status and organization were at last - in May - given to six journalists, of whom one - and he not the least - was an American.

Four photographers and cinematographers, gallant workers all, moved up and down the front taking every characteristic feature of the war. Finally in August 1916 a great artist was given a commission to immortalize with pencil and etchings the battlefields of the Somme and the men who fought over them. Propaganda became a blessed word; and no longer were any of its genial officials known as the Proper-geese!

The result of it all was that a steady flow of confidence in the sense and solidity of the national effort carried away the old stagnant flood of shallow optimism. We began to trust in British excellence, rather than in imagined and imaginary German decay.

Yet the war itself moved not at all. In June we were to see in the field how powerful for attack as well as defence the enemy still remained. Once more - was it for the last time? - the semicircle of Ypres was a charnel. The tale of what the Canadians endured and how they afterwards retaliated has been told not once, but many times; but the tale has always been of the infantry, never of the field gunner. Yet the reverse was a gunners' battle; and this is how a gunner described his experiences in what he called the third battle of Ypres. The whole tale would fit the second battle in spite of our multiplication of guns and munitions.

"My battery had been for months in a nice 'cushy' place, invisible except by aeroplanes, and undetected by them.

"From the observation post, well tee'd up among the rooks, you could overlook the whole plain and trace out, even with the naked eye, a mile or so of serpentine trenches. You could see without using the excellent telescope how our shrapnel broke over the little German salient, and when called upon you telephoned back with the utmost satisfaction, 'O.K.' or 'Carry on.'

"Then when life was most pleasant and, under the touch of leafy June, the O.P. had assumed all the qualities of a summer-house, news came that the battery was ordered to shift to a place uncomfortably near sea-level, where there are neither hills nor leaves, where nothing is below you, where the standard method of concealment is that of an eel in the mud. More than the worst was realized. The battery was attached to another unit holding a most uncomely piece of the front, and it was to be the forward battery.

"Directly you arrived in the place, even at night, you had the feeling that eyes were observing you. You were the mouse to the owl or the lark to the hawk. At first the weather was foul, with a high wind, and the unpleasantness was felt to be a protection, though no one, except the major, who had been in the district before, quite realized to the full the compensations of foul weather. But it was not long before every one knew as much as the major on this head.

"Three days after the arrival the weather cleared, and the Germans began a slow but persistent hammering at our trenches, and in spite of a sausage balloon right opposite, which looked full of eyes, reprisals from our guns were demanded. Members of this advanced position felt a horrible certainty that this 'liverspot in the sky,' as some one called the balloon, was marking down every flash and every puff of smoke; that the site of the battery was being fixed down on a large-scale chart with cold accuracy, reaching to fractions of a millimetre.

"The only consolation was high approval of the shooting from the advanced observer. By the next day comparative cheerfulness was restored. Some one was arguing that there was a good deal after all in the theory of protective coloration, and that you did not really need cover when the whistle of an approaching shell broke the thread of the argument. Being men of experience, they all knew that the shell was meant for them. The selected target is usually self-conscious and has more than a professional desire to know how good the shooting is. This noise topped the centre gun of the battery like a driven partridge over a hedge, and was converted into a visible object as it struck earth some forty yards behind.

"'By the Lord Harry - registered!' said the major, and looked wickedly at the balloon as if he could see the creature in it putting a blue pencil spot where the shell exploded before telephoning down to his guns that no further registering shots were needed. At all times the hate of a gunner for the sausage is a thing beyond expression. Now and again, in spite of discipline, it breaks bounds. The temptation to let loose at one of the hated balloons worked so strongly in two young officers that they suggested in a meek and inferential manner that they might be permitted to take a single field-gun forward to a hiding spot they knew of, and to work their will on this uncomely and ill omened bird. Needless to say, the idea was not approved.

"So the thing was still there, inquisitive and menacing as ever, the next day when the slow bombardment and the tentative reprisals broke out into an artillery battle as hot as the gunners on both sides could make it. Every one knew this was at last a real battle, wiping out all experiences of the younger men and most of the older. Even the balloon was forgotten. Every gun was firing as fast as the men could sling in the shells and the cleaners work. There was scarcely time to listen to the voice down the megaphone bellowing at the closest range short series of mathematical figures. One of the guns in this advanced battery grew so hot that it seized and could be used no more till it cooled down. The gun pits so filled with empty shells that nothing could be done till space was made. Why every one was not deaf and blind long ago it was impossible to say.

"But that day there were louder noises than the battery made itself. It had indeed been registered by the enemy. Any observer from a few hundred yards' distance would have said that not so much as a mouse was left alive within a hundred yards of any of the guns. Were the guns, then, shooting automatically? For continuously one or other of the quartet never ceased to fire at its fullest speed. The gunners themselves had no brain or senses to observe or consider the miracle.

34

"A very heavy shell - was it a 12 inch or only an 8 inch? - exploded close against the emplacement of the left-hand gun. Instantly, so it seemed, the whole team collapsed and vanished. The shock to the air was enough to destroy life. Nevertheless presently a lieutenant and a sergeant found themselves fit and well - two men at any rate capable of serving the gun. They carried on. And as they went on firing, slowly but very methodically, in a state of dazed tension, gradually one by one bandaged and deafened helpers came back. The vast explosion, which might have served for a considerable episode in extinction of a world, had neither damaged the gun nor killed a single man. Possibly it had saved the lives of half the battery, for from this moment the enemy shells ceased to wallow like pigs in the trough.

"Coming back to realization of smaller things than the end of the world, some one noticed that the sausage had vanished. The light was seen to be bad. It was not only the smudge of dust and smoke which obscured distant things. The atmosphere was different, visibility low; and the German is not very fond of blind shooting, except at certain crises and for very definite attacks. The sullen noise of our guns, mixed with occasional bursts, continued through the evening and into the night; but the height of battle and strain was over. The battery had done its part. So had the ammunition carriers, the living and the dead."

When all the story was told and the battery moved to another resting-place it seemed a thing incredible in the retrospect that men and guns, save a small minority, had come through alive and in working order. In each of their persons the gunners felt that a miracle had been wrought.

Like miracles were wrought many score of times in the Somme battle; but then always and everywhere our gunners knew themselves to be the masters, and to possess the mastery of observation.

An even more furious artillery onset was directed against the Londoners, who proved, to the surprise of many, among the best troops we have; and the Vimy ridge for a while surpassed Ypres. The Germans possess what is known as "the travelling circus" a body of expert gunners who travel at will along the front, concentrating on any desired piece of line. They are used for the sake of producing moral as well as material results. A German band heralds their arrival, announcing to all and sundry that the enemy is about to have the worst time in his life; and their arrival is always hailed with cheers. This circus arrived on the Vimy ridge, as desolate a spot as the front has to show, in early June. It had come to add the final flourish to the local artillery. Rather more shells than usual had been falling round our trenches and batteries, but nothing much was thought of it; for "registering" of this nature is almost continuous along the lines. But this registering had more behind it. Early in the afternoon shells and gas shells began to rain over a number of our batteries; and a few batteries were selected for a tornado. While this scattered anti-battery bombardment was in progress one of our generals mounted an observation post - there is none better in France - to survey the scene. He had hardly reached the spot when on a sudden the whole of our front trench began to smoke as if some one had lit a swathe of dry hay. He watched the smoke and fire run along the line with diabolic accuracy. Shells of three calibres - 77, 4.5, and 5.9 - fell so thickly and with such precision that within a few minutes the whole scene was obliterated in dust and smoke; the cloud came down and enveloped both the valley and the slope of the hill. So thick was it that no one ever knew at what moment the German infantry advanced. No single Londoner retired, but every man bore it out "even to the edge of doom." A very, very few were taken prisoner. None returned to tell the tale. They had suffered the most thorough and scientific bombardment yet known in history, and it was associated with counter battery work, exceptionally wide and precise. The enemy had used his superior position to the highest advantage. He could see all that we did. We could see little that he did, and in this war observation is everything.

But even on the morrow of that action, by which the German won a mile of useful trench, our men had no feeling (as after the second battle of Ypres) that we were outgunned. Everywhere the sense grew that the enemy was to suffer as we had suffered; and their hopes were justified. At Vimy for the last time the German guns mastered us. For the last time (for many months at any rate) the offensive, the attack, the will to attack was with the enemy. The tide was on the turn. The highest wave had broken. How nearly we had been engulfed, not once or twice, we can scarcely imagine; we shall perhaps never know.

From the beginning of the year we had struggled hard to win the mastery of the air, and seemed to be near success, when for a short space a set-back was threatened. Suddenly one day half the world began to hear terrible tales of the Fokker, a German plane credited with super alpine powers of climbing and unimaginable speed. Many of our pilots themselves feared this new machine, and had kept a nervous eye on it some while before the public knew the name. The type, which was fast and of high speed, had been multiplied by the enemy for purely defensive purposes. Fokkers continually patrolled his lines, usually at a great height - 12,000, even 15,000, feet - sometimes singly, sometimes in groups. From this altitude they dived at hostile craft, not infrequently striking their victim and seldom themselves suffering loss, thanks to their method. They defended; they seldom transgressed their own boundaries, and rarely pursued a duel. The past master in this defensive art was the famous Immelmann, who was to meet his fate, over his favourite locality, near Lille, from a young South African, whose first victim he was. But the Fokker was no lasting menace. The patrolling methods were learnt and answered; and the machine itself, when captured, proved less powerful than it had appeared. Our mastery of the air was never so, great as during the preparations for the Somme, two months after Immelmann's highest success.

When the great battle approached we had some real superiority on every plane. Our miners, a hundred feet into the chalk at Fricourt and Boiselle, proved a higher quality of nerve than the German, just as our airmen won the prize of observation by superior daring in the upper planes of air. Our gunners were superior in numbers, if not as yet in skill; and had control of more shells, if many of them were rather inferior in quality. The infantry were short of experience, especially the younger officers, but they excelled the enemy in personal daring at close quarters, at least as much as he excelled them in the skilful use of position for machine-guns and automatic rifles. We were ready, or nearly ready, for the Great Adventure.

PART II

CHAPTER I
THE COMING EVENT

M ANY PEOPLE STILL believed and feared that the desolate monotony of the war was permanent . Blind and muddy it had been, blind and muddy it would continue. But before May was out most of us who had freedom to visit all parts of the front, from the marshes of Ypres to the pretty woods of Vaux on the Somme, knew that our cumulative sense of excitement was justified. We knew the great battle was in preparation along the south part of our line, the pleasant country of hill and dale below Arras, which we had taken over from the French. In the last week of June the expectation of a great adventure touched the people at home as well as the men in the trenches. To his horror, one of our generals concerned with the organization of the battle received a letter from his people in England asking whether the attack was to be on 28th June or 1st July! In modern warfare a great attack can scarcely be hidden. A thousand and more guns are not easily concealed, even if they do not "register"; and the movement of stores and troops is "a thing imagination boggles at." Exactly where the coming blow was to be struck was harder to tell, though many knew. The Germans believed the attack would be delivered on a front stretching roughly from Arras to the Ancre, and appear to have harboured no suspicion that it would extend to the Somme, much less south of the Somme. For ourselves, while we advertised the approach of battle, we strove to hide its whereabouts. The artillery bellowed from one end to the other. You could not find a five-mile reach of country where stretches of German wire - thick, brutal, indestructible stuff it is - was not uprooted and scattered in aimless coils. A fury of raids broke out; and night after night at a dozen places in the line our men penetrated the German trenches, sometimes finding the enemy alert and the trench full, and fighting hard, more often returning with one or two prisoners from a thin garrison.

Never perhaps in its history has our nation vibrated with such sense of expectancy as on the eve of 1st July. The great event cast more than a shadow before it; rather the shaft of a searchlight. The clamour of guns shouting from Ypres to Montauban filled the ears of all who lived along the 90 miles of trench line, within 20 or even 40 miles of it. The noise was spreading over the inhabited world; and all whose senses were in order could scent the battle from afar.

In France itself, among our army, and, indeed, the enemy's, excitement touched a height impossible to gauge. For several weeks I had felt like a man who watches a flood rise to the edge of a bank and knows that the moment must soon come when it will break bounds, perhaps shatter the bank, and in all certainty bring the ruin of thousands and ten thousands of lives. The world was big with fear and hope. Oppression and excitement alternated. Perhaps the observer with nothing to do but look and wait realized the imminence more than the soldiers; though he felt it less. He was not kept awake for three, four, five nights by alarms of gas, the regulation of his own gas, and the thunder of the guns. He had not before him that prospect of that intense moment when the trenches are packed, and every man has his eye on the watch and quivers with unendurable expectancy for the second when he must scramble over the parapet, and across the open pursue the advancing curtain of his shells.

Nevertheless, though his own body is safe enough, and instead of the soldier's alternative of death or glory he nurses only a certain shame that he can claim no lot or share in the great day, the observer who has watched the waters rise, who knows the plans, who has crept forward to view the length and breadth of the field, is conscious of feelings very near the soldier's, though in a sense impersonal. I had visited forward observation posts and various front trenches day after day with accumulating sense of the immensity of the issue and the inevitable sacrifice. Nor was it all foretaste. The field-gun battery I passed near X lost three of its gunners in the interval while I was visiting the trench beyond and watching the havoc of our own shells. The shadow of the coming event was over the enemy; and most of the guns that he was not afraid to disclose he set to counter battery work. The tension was never a moment released. Soldiers, N.C.O.'s, regimental officers, and staffs all felt as men feel at the start of a race: not fearful, but tense. An almost sleepless army quivered at the leash.

The raids that preceded and accompanied the five days' bombardment from 26th to 30th June were of varying success; the Highland Light Infantry, attacking near Angres, north of Souchez, claimed the most successful. They entered the trenches without loss, fought in them against numerous enemy for an hour round midnight, and returned with forty-six prisoners. Below this little triumph tailed down a succession of raids, including some failures. The Germans were ready and quick. But the general endeavour was so successful that, we gained identifications of every German division from North to South, with information of much utility in all the subsequent fighting.

From prisoners and other sources we catch many glimpses of the German mind during these days. Special orders were issued and encouragement given. The men were told that if they held up the enemy in the coming attack, the war was won. It was a final despairing effort of the Allies, who would sue for peace when they failed, and the good German soldiers would return to their homes before Christmas. Every man was to hold to the death.

On our own side little or nothing was said directly to the men till the very eve. Then many memorable speeches were made, some memorably good, some memorably bad. The men liked best the speeches most full of information and least full of exhortation. They listened with delight to the tally of shells which had passed over them on the way to the Germans: so many hundred of so many tons, per hour for so many hours, with other charming statistics. Listening to the oratory, subalterns of a classical bent and some imagination almost thought themselves back into the time of Homer, when heroes killed each other with their mouth before coming to sterner blows.

One of the great subjects of discussion at regimental headquarters was whether it was better to be in the attack or in support. Most preferred the attack on the ground that supports get more than half the shelling and little of "the fun." A short while before, I spent many hours in the front trenches by Gommecourt, where every one was lamenting the order that the battalion was to be held in reserve. And how safe, how quiet the trench seemed. A number of us looked over the parapet and stared at the German lines with confidence. The only sign of Germans was an occasional burst of 4.2 shrapnel at an extraordinary height in the air, whence it rained down innocuously. It was hard to believe that crossing the parapet could be so deadly a pursuit, that presently wave after wave would sweep across that ugly interval among the maddest racket that ever man conceived. Yet at this point the enemy was preparing the very hub of his defence.. Several new batteries were parked under the peaceful trees in front. New wire was fixed in the nights. German aeroplanes made efforts to discover the 9.2 howitzers which had registered on Gommecourt Wood, that sharp salient which we faced on the west and - at greater trench distance - on the north and south-west.

The serenity did not appear to be much diminished when one visited the O.P. and could observe the fall of the occasional shells from the same heavy howitzers raising great pillars of cloud among the belt of rather scrubby trees in front. Fighting of this sort is always unreal, because blind. The unreality was reduced almost to farce when one of our airmen, much beloved, though by name unknown to our infantry, began to turn Catherine wheels among the fleecy billows of shrapnel smoke over the German lines. War? Impossible. Not even a passable imitation.

Yet most of war was there. I heard even the rattlesnake rattle of our machine-guns, which at capricious moments raked some bunches of trees in front, searching for German observers. One at any rate shot with effect. A straight black object, thought to be a telescope, was clearly seen to fall from the upper boughs of a beech. All this was in mid June. From 25th June war was tangible enough even in front trenches, where the men, though victims to a legion of false rumours, are always calm and quiet. And hopes ran high. The news was good. In spite of waterspouts of rain, we were the full masters of No Man's Land. The news of the lightning raids that had broken out from Ypres to Fricourt was cheered all along the line. Wherever you went you were asked for more details of the H.L.I, and their forty-six prisoners, and of the savage night-time fight of the Oxford and Bucks raiders along the enemy's parapets. A few deserters had come over, apologizing for their desertion on the ground that our artillery had cut them off for three whole days from meat and drink. And all the time, steadily, though never in hurricane fashion, our heavy guns dispatched their express trains overhead with a most comforting roar and rattle. To sit in a trench as I sat day after day (and incidentally to watch the mortars explode in the German lines) while these vast shells were coursing to remote and unseen targets gave an amazing sense of security. Their clamour is so distinctly localized and so long continued that you look up constantly with the feeling that they must be visible. But the faith of the man in the trenches for Lazy Lizzie or Grandmother needs no sight, though the long-distance monsters now first began to find a very strong rival in the more visible trench mortars, whose range and quality and quantity had suddenly increased.

The truth seemed to be established that the munitions campaign had reached fruition at last. The German, of course, was answering, and was well supplied. He shelled our lines very heavily in several places; but he had himself never yet indulged on this front in so widely extended a use of artillery.

The extensive as against the intensive method was for the first time - so it seemed - on trial, and (without attaining any crucial results) it had clearly much agitated the enemy, caused him considerable losses, and left our infantry free to enter his trenches at night here, there, and everywhere.

Some few people conjectured even on the eve of 1st July that the battle was to be a gunners' battle, slowly wearing down the enemy without the use of great forces of infantry. Were not the guns noisy from Ypres to the Somme? But these guessers had not passed new and forward gun emplacements, and entered roomy assembly trenches, and wondered at the mountains of shells stored behind, and marked along the roads the momentum of a moving army.

On 24th June, wherever you moved along the front you saw lines of the enemy's sausage balloons. In them were highly expert photographers, who snapped the flash of our guns from many angles, while observers noted down all manner of information both for the gunners and the higher command. Most of the balloons were at least five miles behind the fighting line; but on days of clear vision you can see at this angle only less well than from an aeroplane skied over the very spot. One of our balloons that I knew well - it was christened Ruddy Rupert - so irritated the Germans that they turned a naval gun - nicknamed Whistling Percy - to the sole work of attacking it. The observer heard the whistle go past him, and was on the point of giving the signal to descend, but forbore on a consideration of probabilities. Whistling Percy was at least eight miles off, and he reckoned that the odds on a hit were at least a thousand to one. So he stayed observing for six hours, while Percies hissed past him with much regularity at ten minute intervals, and he looked with occasional nervousness at his parachute.

On 24th June the sky was populous with these German balloons. From 26th June till the first stages of the Somme battle were over, I never saw an enemy's balloon; and the first that appeared was eleven miles behind the front line. For at dawn on the 25th June our airmen and the French, armed with a new method of offence, set out on a special "sausage campaign"; and so successful was it that within an hour or two six of the enemy's balloons were in flames. Thenceforth none dare ascend; and when at last some courage returned, the balloon was always sent up empty for a while to draw fire. All through the battle our airmen gave proof of high courage and skill in attacking these balloons, which were always defended from the ground both by "Archies" and by machine-guns. One airman pretended to be hit, and tumbled his machine down till he was close to the balloon and at its level. He then set it on fire with a volley and flew away, twisting this way and that, amid a storm of fire.

Our own balloonists met with few accidents, though they approached sufficiently near the lines; and some of the most curious escapes recorded in the war are associated with the balloons. One was caught in a thunderstorm, and under the pressure dragged its engine and winch, which upset in a ditch. One of the observers attempted to jump out in his parachute but was caught in the rigging. At this crisis the gas escaped very rapidly from the envelope; but so powerful was the tempest that it filled out the umbrella of the parachute, which now bore a great part of the weight of the basket, and this little extra force of buoyancy was just enough to slow the fall sufficiently. Neither occupant was badly hurt.

The wire of another balloon, struck by an aeroplane, penetrated half through the wing. It seemed a certainty that the aeroplane must crash and the wire break; but the impossible happened. The aeroplane, with its engine running lightly, circled round and round on the pivot of the sloping wire, all the while steadily slipping down. When at last it reached the ground, its release occupied several hours of hard work. The danger was that the wire would break when the flattened part was released and the balloon float off. The motor which winds the wire, and if need be draws the balloon along, had been pulled over on its side. In the sequel the two machines and all the crews came off with nothing worse than temporary wounds.

All the history of the balloons illustrates the best known quality of the British nation. The war was a year old before we paid much attention to the subject. The steady multiplication was one of the scores of signs of the coming event; and when the moment came, we had more balloons than any other combatant. It was a standard amusement to count them. The longer you looked the more you saw. They seemed to grow on the view like stars on a photographic lens. I counted twenty-two on the morning of 1st July, and have made the sum on occasion to thirty-two, a sky-pointer to the line and direction of the trenches.

For the time, the enemy was beaten in the air. He fought half blind, and did not recover till November, when his new double-engined plane and a great national effort recovered for him, not equality, but some measure of adequate competition.

The outbreak of our continuous and heavy shelling and our capture of the air synchronized with a certain weakening of the enemy's forces, opposite the French if not opposite us. The nth Bavarian Regiment and the 22nd Reserve Corps left for the Russian front, and the 10th Corps was sent east from the Champagne. In all eight divisions disappeared. Very soon the migration was reversed, and troops radiated to the hub of the Somme from north and south as well as east - naval troops from north of Ypres and Bavarians from Verdun. The thoughts of all Germany hung on the battle of the Somme.

CHAPTER II
JULY 1:
FROM THE HILL

O N THE NIGHT of 30th June, in a little room with windows carefully closed, the hour of the great attack was whispered and the rough scheme of battle unfolded. From the night and morning of 1st July, when through the velvety mist of summer we stormed fifteen miles of enemy's fortress, to the dark days of November, when what was failure at first was wrenched into full success, day after day without intermission a group of us watched British soldiers fighting the battle of the Somme. For myself, sometimes muddy trenches, sometimes hill-tops carpeted with almost alpine flora, sometimes the open muddle of the field, a ruined wall, a treetop, an aeroplane, have all served as watch-towers for the panorama of battle. For week after week the memory of each day has been a memory of a smoking landscape and intolerable noise, of prisoners, of wounded men, of dead men on the field and behind it. Every friend you sought anywhere was busy in some way with the work of war. The doctor, without a moment's intermission from the matter in hand, talked of common home affairs while he squeezed shrapnel bullets out of a soldier's back, as you could shell peas out of a pod; and he stands as a symbol of this incredible life wherein all men take war as a matter of course and only outside things as events. A war correspondent, as any other observer, though he touches much that shocks every sense, deals chiefly with the milder side of war. His experience is of its breadth rather than its depth, yet he sees its extent, its complexion, its variety of feature, as perhaps few others see them. He may visit, and does visit, the whole field. I have known it from Nieuport dunes, from the desolate ramparts of Ypres to the pretty woods of Vaux by the marshes of the Somme. He has acquaintance with battle from near and far, from observation points perhaps 800 or 1000 yards behind the charging infantry to the end of a telephone that is the eye of the Headquarters staff or the gunner major. When battle is over he may visit the field at a leisure but mildly troubled by occasional shells.

Waiting for the battle of the Somme was like waiting at the start of a race in which one had no share but an intensity of interest. When a general came at midnight and shut door and window with care and whispered the hour of attack and the plan of campaign, excitement was almost intolerable. But the whole army now knew that the long tension was to finish within a few hours. The raids and pettish shelling over Flanders down to the Somme and across it were to be over and done with. They were in some sort a battle and preparation for battle; but in essentials a mere flurry and flourish, a caracole before the charge.

All was now to condense into the passion of personal contest within the compass of a narrower span. At a point within that span I stood with a few others, watches in hand, at the dawn of that perfect summer morning. The birds began to feed and chirp in the charlock by the trench's edge. The low rays of the sun ricochetting off the surface of the valley mist baffled all endeavours to penetrate the mystery of the battle-field, which spread before us, and indeed around us, in a spacious arc.

No more than a modicum of sullen, capricious sounds betokened the crisis. Little was to be seen anywhere. There were neither night fireworks nor day tumult. For myself, I was watching the ugly bulk of one of the huge sausage balloons rise ponderously over the trees behind me, in very poor imitation of the larks, when the hour long and nervously awaited struck as suddenly as if it were unexpected.

A year of anticipation would not have prevented or lessened the surprise. The mist was burst by a shock that no one can attempt to describe. All I know about my own sensations is that I had none left after five minutes. The monster of war had no features. A Niagara of sound poured ceaselessly, in volume incomprehensible, without distinctions. The orchestra was making not music but noise in harmony; and no one was musician enough to distinguish the parts.

In this blur I had only one friend to cling by. A giant gun far away to my right was at work enfilading a German trench to my left; and as its comet projectile churned through the air I could hear distinctly the whistling note of its passage, the one individual, separate, palpable thing in an ocean, an atmosphere of dull, shapeless thunder-noise. It was neither painful nor glorious, this part of the battle as I saw it, or rather heard it; but just a dull, local opiate, killing sensation, though leaving consciousness.

After awhile the mind recovered and the senses became acclimatized. By a quite steady progression the mist thinned and rose. I could pick out batteries that I knew and watch their stabs of flame and puffs of smoke. By seven o'clock you were quite sure that the flashes were not, as for a while you had feared, the bursting explosion from the enemy's howitzers; for the flame from the gun-muzzle is horizontal, from the high-explosive shell vertical.

At 7.15, so clear were the batteries, flashing here, there, and everywhere, almost as numerous and thick as tents in a camp, that you were amazed the enemy had not marked out every single pit for instant destruction; but as yet not a shell came near them. The German gunners could not spare time, it seemed, for the batteries, when infantry were massing in the trenches. Nor could they see as our army could see.

One after another our balloons had risen to the full height of their tether in a long line stretching quite out of sight. Their kite-tails streamed to the eastward, advertising the arrival of a good, steady west wind about to blow Heaven knows what fumes and smoke and dust and ashes from the front to the back trenches of the enemy's first line. But as yet the observers could look clear into the cockpit of battle: into the village of Fricourt, into Serre, into Beaumont-Hamel, where every leaf had been blown from the shattered trees by our lire, and every shelter and dugout was a mangled mess.

The highest thing I saw in the place was one ten foot wall or so; and the trenches running into it looked like the first shale-tips of a deserted mine. And our army had yet better eyes than the balloons. Right over my head, against the clear background of a fleecy layer of cloud, a whole squadron of our aeroplanes, almost cloud-high, but pencilled in marvellous distinctness against the cirrus flakes, flew as the crow flies, direct for their target. Argus-eyed, and with more than a Cyclops' voice, they saw and shouted back the news of the guns' precision, untouched by the monstrous tumult below. They left the dappled puffs of shrapnel in beaded ropes behind them, as a fish leaves bubbles, till soon you could not tell which was cloud and which was smoke.

At 7.30 the sights of the upper air were forgotten and quite obscured by such an earth-born cloud as might accompany the conflagration of a forest. Column after column of thick smoke rose and spread and floated forward from our trenches towards the enemy. Bullets of all sorts hummed and whistled. That inhuman, oscillating bullet of the German rifle and machine-gun and the round bullets of the shrapnel, some of them sprinkled with phosphorus, threaded the woof of the cloud; but it was blind shooting. The cloud played its part, and many a man who left his trench behind its cover owes his life to the beneficent obscurity. Nevertheless, many of the men would have liked to charge in full day for sheer pride of manhood and zest of clean sight. The "Up-and-at-'em" spirit was strong in our army that summer morning.

The scene at night had been stranger. Then, unexpected as it may sound, you saw more and heard less. Instead of a misty monotone you watched continuously the flash of guns and blaze of explosions over twenty or thirty miles of country, and the star shells stippled out the line of the trenches. Since Midsummer Day we had turned night into day on the method of King Mycerinus, though his Egyptian grove was never lit so splendidly as these dour lines of trenches and ruined houses.

No half-hour of the night was allowed to sink into its native gloom. No minute while I watched was lit by less than some hundred flashes, not reckoning the graceful and abiding star shells, which had all the semblance of a cosmic or celestial calm among the impish snap and flicker of bomb and shrapnel bursts or the thrust of the flash from the gun muzzle. One spot in front of me seemed especially selected as the scene for a spiritual conflict between the two. Every time that the star, pure white and splendid, soared to its summit, alongside its apex, now this side, now that, glinted a trio of red shrapnel sparks, like the wink of a wicked eye; and the festoon of the falling star lit a column of cloud that might have escaped from a mouth of hell.

Away on the right the flicker was so continuous and jerky as to hurt the eyes. It gave the impression of a bad kinematograph film. Farther away all the lights, good and bad, were toned to the harmless expansion of what we call summer lightning, illumining wide stretches of sky and etching the patterns of the clouds.

The great preponderance of trench mortars, at least on our side, during this night fighting dwarfed the noise of battle, and for a part of the time I happened to stand in what the French call a pool of silence, one of those mysterious regions, or perhaps zones, over which the sound passes almost unheard, to strike loudly the drums of ears, it may be, ten or so miles in the rear.

Gorgeous as the scene was in itself, it was a pitiful thing beside the immediate human interest. Moving forward, we overtook some battalions on the march to the trenches. First I heard the rhythmic tramp and muffled noises as of a ghostly army; then distinguished the sway and swing of a brown and lifeless pattern; then, when the figures grew clearer, could count the double company and detect the English quality in the men; yet still I could not shake off the sense of marching with an army of ghosts in the limbo of some other world, for ever seeking to reach that unknown region of stars and thunder.

The lorries rubbing past us in the gloom were like extinct megatheria, colossal and shapeless, but half alive. Noisier beasts, with long snouts and strange modes of progression, moved the other way or were passed as they slept (or was it grazed?) under the trees. They too were on the way to populate this strange country beyond the gloom.

But one did not march far with the men before recovering the sense of human things and proper reality. Gallant fellows, they whistled home-like airs, and on the way to the trench kept a merry heart. A little farther, and even the subdued whistle would be unwise.

One platoon hummed the "Marseillaise" in harmony. "Not a bad tune, the old Mayonnaise," said a listener; and after that the sense of a Stygian limbo could no longer endure. You were almost at home and altogether among actualities. A most English regiment was on the march at midnight down a country road in the hope of "bumping the Boche." A merry heart goes all the way. The celestial and devilish lights were a "Brock's benefit for the Boche," not a mystic Aurora Borealis or a mythical grove by the Nile.

Your master thought now was, "Thank goodness that 80 per cent, of those flashes come from us, not the enemy" and the only splendour that mattered the turn of a card was the splendour of victory.

Finer spirits never deserved a heartier Godspeed or merited more of their country.

Such a view of battle gives no hint of the fortune of the day; and men in high places were as ignorant as we. No true news was known by anyone for hours. One division could not tell its neighbour division where the men were or how far the trenches were won. Flashes of hope, half-lights of expectation, hints of calamity only penetrated the smoke and dust and bullets that smothered the trenches.

The tension was unendurable. The telephones, the carrier pigeons, the guesses of direct observers, the record of the runners, the glimpses of the airmen, all combined could scarcely penetrate the fog of war. The wounded who struggled back from German trenches themselves knew little.

Those of us who were gazing from the misty hill hurried away to hear the official news, and, still unrelieved by certain tidings, pushed forward into the hurly-burly of the corridors of battle down in the valley. There the great events of the battle stood out quite distinct, though no one could go bail for any one point of evidence. We had galloped across the Montauban trenches, were in the edges of Mametz, and forcing our way up the hill west of Fricourt. All the rest of the battle still lay in the fog.

CHAPTER III
JULY 1:
FROM THE FIELD

E VEN IN THE trenches the dawn of 1st July seemed calm and sweet, at least till the full chorus of the guns opened at 6.30. The field on both sides of the line was dissembled under a soft mist, above which here and there a high spire or lofty tree just peeped out. I could catch now and then the glint of the sun on the golden body of the Virgin, battered by German guns from her upright poise, and now holding out from the red tower of Albert the little figure of the Child Jesus, a symbol of many things not yet come to pass. The French inhabitants say that when the two fall the war will be over. To all who pass - and half the Army has passed - that figure suggests some of the most moving thoughts and memories in their life or in literature. Even in the intensity of the excitement of that morning a looker-on found himself muttering that poignant Virgilian line:

"Tendentesque manus ripae ulterioris amore."

It was a common experience of men waiting in the trenches for the supreme moment that their minds went back to little inconsequent things. They were too highly strung to have control of that part of their mind not directly concerned with action. The waiting was hard. Many officers had not slept for many nights. If they could have surmounted the discomfort of the trench and shut their ears to the intolerable artillery and their eyes to the shifting lights loosed by a nervous enemy, they had still a multitude of duties forbidding sleep. In some places gas was released; and every emission of gas means a score of orders and counter orders depending on the chance of the wind and weather.

With innumerable batteries in action it was inevitable that here and there a gun should fire short and endanger our own trench. To make sure of the offence and to find the offender is not an occupation to induce sleep. The gunners had less chance of sleep even than the infantry officers, and their strain was the greater during the night hours. But the brunt of war is always borne by the regimental officer. His duties are most insistent, and he runs the supreme risk. In preparing to charge a trench his greatest fear is to lose direction. How little this trouble is understood outside the Army; and the fault lies with the scale of the maps. The lines look so regular and the rival lines so close together. What is there to do but cross that little gap at all speed? But the gap is neither little nor regular.

At various places on our fifteen miles of front we had front trenches of some length facing north and south, though our general line faced east, and some bits faced slightly west. To ensure the even tenor of the attack the infantry officer must take almost as much trouble with his alignment as the master gunner. In many parts south of Hébuterne, where the trench pattern was more than usually complex, men went out into No Man's Land during the night to play the surveyor and lay down tape or chalk lines for the direction of the troops. Perhaps excessive precautions were taken in the arrangement of details. Nothing seemed to be forgotten, even to the laying of waterpipes up to points about to be conquered.

The interval between the trenches varied as much as the angle. North of Gommecourt a brigade dug a new trench in the course of a single night, and dug it almost without casualties; but the interval was still 500 yards. Opposite them the enemy played a strange trick in reply. He built a new trench, one end resting on a peak in his own line, the rest breaking new ground nearer to us. A little while later a superior officer coming to inspect, condemned the new trench, and ordered the German regiment that built it to fill it up again!

All these things were photographed by airmen, watched by observers from all sorts of peepholes, and set down on the war maps. The distances were wider than most intervals in the north; the 5 yards in the Arras suburbs, or the 40 at Kemmel. The troops had 200, 300, 400, even 500 yards to cross at one place or another, the distance diminishing from north to south. The widest gap was at Gommecourt, where we had the better of the hill, the narrowest about Fricourt, where both trenches descended each from its supporting hill into the long valley. In front of Montauban, where we shared the ridge with the Germans, the distance was about 150 yards.

The scheme was precise, mathematical, so worked out by the higher command as to give the least trouble to soldier or regimental officer. So thorough was the previous work that every man knew exactly what he had to do, at the start and at the finish. Each wave was to "go over" with the men spaced so many yards apart. Just so many yards were to divide each of the first four waves. The several lines were specially armed and instructed for peculiar work: for seizing a trench, for occupying it, for defending it and for supplying the defenders. Such and such a wave was to capture such a line of objective, in some cases the fourth, in some the first or second line; and such others were to follow after, "go through" and seize such a further objective. Artillery fire was synchronized exactly with these infantry movements, at first by time, later perhaps by signal, as the French do.

The plans were complete. Corps generals who had worked day and night had taught a great army their plans, and they themselves had little to do but await the issue and the first news with what patience they could command. One of them walked to and fro from his study to the chateau garden through a window shattered to fragments by the shock of our heavy guns. Within the trenches some 100,000 men, strung to the highest pitch of nervous intensity, and yet calm and humorous to the last, awaited the supreme moment. One of the divisions engaged - and in the hottest place - had already made an immortal name, for its bravery and its losses, in the landing of Gallipoli; and already the deeds are recorded in a form worthy of the courage by Mr. Masefield, with the restraint and force of Kinglake or Napier and with more than the simple charm of either. When this ill-fated and glorious division faced the Germans across the wires and holes of No Man's Land in Picardy it rejoiced in the absence of all the peculiar terrors of Gallipoli. Its task was bare and simple, almost crude.

As the seconds ticked on in the midst of a sulky bombardment every officer looked at his wrist watch not once but a hundred times, and from his watch to his men's faces. "Do I look as green as I feel," thought one subaltern, "and shall I funk it?" Later he was astounded to remember how natural and cool he had been. He was only conscious of sharpened senses. The whereabouts of a machine gun he knew by instinct, and led his men under cover with the tact of an Indian. His company won to their full objective without extreme loss, perhaps because the wrist watch he consulted so carefully, so nervously, was a second or two fast. For the first over the parapet fared best. The battle was probably opened in front of Auchonvillers, where a fast watch or over-eager spirit sent the men over the parapet ten seconds too soon. Some few fell from our own shells; but so close did the battalion move to the curtain of our shells that the enemy had not raised his head and the machine-guns were not in position. How differently fared the Newfoundlanders who were withheld till three hours had passed.

It is easy to understand why this should be. Every battle-field in the battle of the Somme disappears into blackness and smoke, but no field ever so reeked with fumes as the German lines on 1st July. We released enormous clouds of smoke that had no object save to conceal. Mingling with the light mist they floated slowly down the south-west wind, taking away the landscape and wiping out the figures of advancing troops. Within the mist, as if it boiled up with its own internal energy, rose the spouts of black and earthy reek from the heavy shells, and crowning these spreading columns and whorls of rising smoke, the little shrapnel clouds and winks of flame coped the gloom with a sort of beauty.

The effect of the clamour and tumult is incommunicable in words and impossible to remember in sensation; but the most terrible noise was not from the guns. At the moment when our artillery lengthened their fuses and lifted the fire to allow our men to charge the rattle of the German machine guns that burst out at our charging troops absolutely drowned the artillery. Compare the size of the cannon and the detonation of a shell with the little pop of a machine-gun, and you will reach some idea of the volume of the fire that British soldiers faced without wincing, for the sake of home and humanity and to kill the creed of a nation that believes in war.

Other noises competed. Our trench mortars, of which much, too much, had been expected, broke through the volume of the heavier artillery, firing in some cases so fast that four shells from one mortar were in the air together. Though some mortars burst, and some jammed, the mortars wrought much havoc, and the sight of these spinning cascades of shells cheered the men to the point even of laughter.

One other sound there was. At the Hawthorn Redoubt, built at the peak of a German salient below Hébuterne, and at a trench maze outside the village of Boiselle, two mines were blown of a depth and volume never before attempted. Their explosion dwarfed the smoke clouds and the great shell explosions, though the noise was almost dull and commonplace. It appeared as if a line of sepia oaks grew while you looked, and as quickly as they sprouted to the size of trees again spread out to the breadth of a forest. In all the immensity of this day nothing else compared with these explosions. They had the effect of a cosmic event, as if the gods were sharing in this mortal ploy.

Was ever a more gigantic signal given to a waiting soldiery?

The advance took up the quality of the signal. It was slow, splendid, majestic, not muddled or muddied or confused, but calm and dignified as in a review. The high-strung nerves were disguised in dignity, and the assault took on the semblance of a procession. The waves went forward geometrically in one, two, three, four parallel lines. Even north of Gommecourt, where success was least and supports were least successful in keeping time, in emerging to the moment, the first waves reached the enemy's trench in a clean formation; and as they marched by the salient of Gommecourt Wood groups of Germans ran out with hands in the air, surrendering to the threat. It was no wonder. Their holes and trenches were almost macadamized by bits of our heavy shells. But no battle plan ever yet survived the shock of personal contact, of the hand-to-hand struggle; and no modern battle keeps a clear pattern when two artilleries cross one another in rival festoons.

Within a few minutes design was lost. Troops, which had known the individual fighting of Gallipoli, again saw that salvation depended on each man's effort; and just as no one had faltered at the outset when they marched as on parade, so now no one struggled back, but every man went forward to the place appointed. In a matter-of-fact way one company, reduced to a remnant by the time the trench was taken, set to work, in literal obedience to previous orders, to form stores of their own and the enemy's bombs at due and proper places in the trench. Each man took up his allotted task according to the division of labour as he had learnt the principle overnight. For some of the duties no one was left, for some, one or two; but when a man had an allotted task, to that at once he set his hand. While he was doing this amid the muddled heaps of earth, and among the bodies of the dead and wounded, he was often quite surrounded by the enemy, a prisoner almost alone among a crowd. But he had his work to do. If he had reached the spot he was to "consolidate," he consolidated, and, though alone, sent up a signal to say he was there.

Staff officers and observers behind were peering through the smoke and confusion for evidence of the progress of the day, and almost all decided that things were going well. They caught sight of the signals everywhere; and though telephones were broken, the evidence of a solid advance seemed sufficient. In a sense the first news they sent to the headquarters of their units was exactly accurate. *Everywhere along the whole front our men reached and passed the German trenches.* It is hard to believe that such a feat was possible over so wide a front against an enemy fortified to the limit of his native thoroughness and forewarned exactly of the time and place.

For the Germans looked to this battle as definitely as the Allies. Every man was ordered to hold out to the death. Were he alone among a multitude he was to die fighting for the glory of the Fatherland and the peace of the world. A thorough and ingenious system of defence was organized and practised, and every effort made to send forward large stores of bombs and cartridges and rations to the fighting trenches. An extra number of officers gathered in the second and reserve trenches, leaving in the front chiefly non-commissioned officers and men.

How far the most successful of the devices of defence was worked out previously, or how far it was accident, we do not altogether know; but we know what happened in those parts of the line where we failed and now have had leisure to poke about among the strong points and trenches and infer the defenders' part from the nature of the defence.

Wherever our infantry departed from instructions it was from excess of zeal. They went too fast and too far in certain places, though perhaps this fault of theirs, if it was a fault, has been exaggerated. The first waves crossed one trench after another without spending time in cleaning them out. That work was to be left to later waves. But the chance was denied them at any rate in the northern section; and the unharmed enemy rose behind the gallant storming parties, sometimes cutting them off, sometimes firing into their backs. For these trenches could hold in concealment untold numbers. At Boiselle and Ovillers the chalk gave opportunity for carving out caverns of any size. The village of Beaumont-Hamel was built out of quarries within the village confines. The famous Y Ravine, 30 feet deep, was scooped into a barracks , with a tunnel running back to the third line. To reach such trenches was one point, to secure them nine points. Not only soldiers with rifles and machine-guns rose behind the first advance. The enemy artillery was grouped as thickly as ours, and when the attack was well on the way, and the battle clearly opened, it opened in volume and with its usual accuracy over our trenches, shrapnel and high explosive together. Orderlies and runners and other messengers were buried again and again on their way forward or back. Observers could not penetrate the smoke and dust. German prisoners, who had surrendered to the first waves, oscillated backwards and forwards, not knowing which danger to face.

But the battle had little uniformity. Even in the midst of the area of failure we won and cleared and held four lines of trenches. One group of a hundred men north of Beaumont-Hamel consolidated the fourth trench, and fought there till four in the afternoon. The enemy was now counter-attacking them from the front and both wings, chiefly with bombs. It was certain death to look over the trench even for a second, as of course the parapet was on the wrong side; and so rifles could scarcely be used. They could only stay where they were and throw bombs half blindly in the direction of the bombs that came. But they held on "till the word went round that there was no more ammunition." No officers were left; and two N.C.O.'s and a few men "met to discuss." They decided to run for it; and thanking their stars for a ground, compact of shell holes, a few of the relic hundred joined their unit before night. One of the lucky men spent an hour of the time within 30 yards of the trench he left, tending a wounded friend. Until it was dark he never could move more than 10 or 12 yards at a time, or in any way other than by little dashes from shell hole to shell hole.

In spite of the intensity of the assault, the severest losses befell those who started later. Our artillery had lifted to more distant targets. The wind had cleared the field of smoke and dust. The German officers had reorganized their men for defence and their artillery observers had a clearer field. The result was that any troops marching forward to answer the call of some distant signal - in Serre or the hollow of Beaumont-Hamel - drew every bullet before ever they reached the protection of an enemy's trench. But they too marched "as on parade" fighting as gloriously as the rest, though they fired no rifle, used no bayonet, and exercised no separate will.

CHAPTER IV
JULY 1:
THE ISSUE OF THE DAY

THE BATTLE OF 1st July was a great victory, though our losses were great, and the success small over more than half the front. We aimed at a deep advance on the right, where we joined the French. On our left, the extreme north of the attack, we sought only to pinch out the little salient of Gommecourt. The measure of success almost marched with the degree of ambition. The utterest failure was north of Gommecourt; the crowning success at Montauban. In one respect the Germans were deceived. They expected the great attack to be centred at Gommecourt and to extend upwards towards Arras as well as down to the river Ancre; and round the centre were accumulated their most powerful batteries. At all parts of the northern attack, from the zero hour of 7.30 A.M. for many continuous hours, the enemy's guns - closely concentrated and of full calibre - set up a triple barrage. Through all these three barrages of intense fire our men marched quite steadily, as if nothing was in the way, as if they were under review. At every step men fell; and our trenches here are very far apart from the German. But our steady, steadfast soldiers, true to the death, paraded in more than decimated numbers through and across the third barrage. The enemy - in their turn heroic - left their trenches, erected machine-guns on the parapets, and the two parties fought one another in the open.

Heroism could no further go. Our men died, and in dying held in front of them enough German guns to have altered the fate of our principal and our most successful advance in the south.

They died defeated, but won as great a victory in spirit and in fact as English history or any history will ever chronicle.

If we leave out the small event north of Gommecourt, the battle may be most easily envisaged as a number of separate actions, for the country is of such a nature that very distinct barriers separated the various divisions and units of attack, though all were united in a well-compacted scheme.

On the peak of Gommecourt itself there was no direct attack; it was left to the ministrations of the artillery. But south of it an immortal battle was fought by London troops whose mettle has been surpassed by none. They fought more or less alone, with a German salient on their left and a sunken road on their right quite cutting them off from immediate contact with the next troops. Opposite them, as against the division on their right, the German defence also was as perfect as defence could be. The dugouts were indestructible. The machine-gunners had the guns in position within a few seconds after our guns lifted. Where we blew a big mine they had already arranged guns to bear on the crater-to-be. The artillery was not less precise. Even through this organization our troops marched without faltering, line after line. The only men who stopped were the dead and severely wounded. But those that crossed a trench - a certain number crossed them - had no chance of holding what they won. They were encircled by machine-guns and bombs, and men rose from dugouts all round. It is the crowning marvel of an incredible battle that men are alive to-day and ready to fight to-morrow who "did the double journey" over the German lines and back.

Yet they won a sort of victory, even these men, for at each trench Germans surrendered, in groups large and small, till the total was considerable, probably several hundred.

But behind both prisoners and captives a barrier of explosive shell dropped like a portcullis. To pass through it untouched was as probable as to pass through a thunderstorm unwetted. Nevertheless the intensity of the intensest barrage varies, and when they took some of their prisoners with them German shells were impartial. Often the captors and a few of the captives came through whole, more crept back "on broken wing"; and every man, whether hale or maimed, knowing that his only avenue to life was through the gate of death, felt that he kept his life by a miracle. So many score of times he might have been killed and was just not killed. And he had found death at every turn - in the advance, in the holding, and in the retreat.

The hours within the German trenches were a battle in themselves. Parties of German grenadiers attacked them from front and both sides. A wounded man or two would hold the mouth of a communication trench against a troop continually recruited. The store of bombs, though increased by those captured from the enemy and used with good effect, progressively failed; and in the sequel, so keenly they fought, it was the failure of supplies, more than the impossibility of their tactical position, that persuaded them to retreat. Their losses were heavy, but they had inflicted heavy losses, and the enemy - on this occasion generous as well as courageous - helped in the saving of the wounded with which No Man's Land was strewn. His stretcher-bearers at one spot brought our wounded even to the edge of our trenches.

South of the Londoners, at a certain remove, was a gap in the infantry fighting, and beyond that gap, at a point in front of Hébuterne, the third engagement was waged. It was sterner than any fought in our annals. I say so with exact knowledge of the names of every battalion in the attack, their losses, their aim, and in the rough how they fared; but a volume would not contain the passion of the true history of their few hours' experience on the morning of 1st July.

The trench line runs at all angles and the ground is up and down. You must not imagine the men as rushing forward levelly, in review formation. It was, of course, a frontal attack, but not on that account simple. The alignment of the men was one of the difficulties. Although the general attack was easterly, some troops moved in a southerly direction - for example, along the valley up to Beaumont-Hamel - and some moved north-east. It says much that in no instance was the direction mistaken or the aim muddled. In open order, some four yards apart, with appropriate distances between the waves, the men advanced punctually to the programme, not running, but marching quickly.

The concentrated cannonade of the enemy's artillery was the worse because the dullness of the weather made counter-battery work difficult for the gunners. "You will never win the village till such and such batteries are knocked out," said a French officer who had himself made an earlier attack. They were not knocked out, yet no single soldier quailed before this fire, or heeded the many gaps. "With what a majesty the British soldier fights." Not a shirker was discovered. Each several line moved "as on parade" to its place in the enemy's lines, starting at the moment our artillery fire lifted.

Against them, as against the Londoners on their left, the front-line trenches were held by large numbers of troops; and as our men came through the curtain of shells they met this other enemy, in force equal to themselves. "Nothing could have stopped us but an opponent of the highest daring, selected and prepared for a battle he thought to be final." So said one of our generals immediately after the battle. The Germans came out of their trenches even in the midst of the final bombardment by our mortars, fixed their machine guns on the parapets or in No Man's Land, and concentrated their fire, some point-blank, some from enfilading angles with skill and coolness. Strong places, which had been crunched to morsels by our artillery, still held armed garrisons. Indeed, from the ruins of Beaumont-Hamel, the strongest of all the villages, a heavy trench mortar fired a few minutes after our artillery lifted.

How any troops reached as far as the German line is hard to believe, but regiment after regiment penetrated to this first and even remoter objective. Middlesex, Devonshire, Worcestershire, Hampshire, Lancashire, South Wales, Dublin, Inniskilling, the Border, and Fusiliers from many quarters fared in this heroic pilgrimage. They entered the German trenches, and carried out their instructions in every detail. The losses varied greatly, owing partly to the nature of the ground, but perhaps more to the accident of the drift of smoke. Moving on a southwest wind in a steady diagonal, it hid some and left others conspicuous. Success depends largely on squaring and timing the artillery fire with the infantry advance, and the progress of the troops must depend on a hundred circumstances beyond previous calculation. Those that are delayed face an enemy no longer worried by shells, and endure the full handicap of the attack. The artillery cannot wait for them or alter the programme or attend to infantry signals which may be bogus or mistaken.

Even the defence had trouble in this way. A small party of our men pushed right through to Serre, a mile at a rush, and sent up signals. The German batteries, thinking we were in possession, at once began - so it is alleged - to shell the village (though at the time it contained a mass of their men and a mere fragment of ours). Here, as elsewhere, probably the one tactical mistake made by our intrepid infantry was a too great eagerness to signal their arrival.

From the medley of conflicting reports, returned by a multitude of observers, it seemed that the most solid success of the advance was south of Beaumont-Hamel over the ridge flanking the Ancre. This important hill descends rapidly to the river on the south and is cut off from the ridge running north and east by a hollow in which flows a tiny brook. Over the slope went the Inniskillings with great dash, and disappeared down into the dust of the valley beyond. On their right the Ulsters had advanced astride the River Ancre, and calling out "No surrender," went right through the blasts of shrapnel and beyond, where three machine-guns, in front and on either flank, caught them. They had even time and spirit to baptize places with good north Irish names: Inniskilling, Omagh, Strabane. They took prisoners and sent them back through the storm. When the prisoners showed fear of the German fire, their shepherd said, "Just you go across, and we'll look after you when you're there."

They organized a defence and broke up with great losses to the enemy a vigorous counter-attack. In spite of the amazing bravery of supporting troops, they were so short of ammunition supplies and so exhausted by fourteen hours of this fighting that the only possible counsel was retirement. And, vast as the losses were, they brought a remnant safe back, running the gauntlet of machine-gunners who had risen from the earth behind them and from strange hiding-places in the trees.

When it was seen that they were through all seemed well. Here was a victory to push home. A strong support was sent forward in their wake, and though the valley and dust swallowed them the signals indicated that the objectives were won. A second support went forward, and later in the day a third.

This third was the Newfoundland Regiment. They advanced over the hill where it sloped to the north-west. The smoke had cleared, and the enemy, so far from being overrun and righting for his life, was now doubly ready. The artillery fire had lifted and the smoke cleared, and the angle of attack became definite. Germans, arisen from caves and dugouts, had cut off the patrols, the groups, the bits of regiments that had penetrated here, there, and everywhere to Serre, to Beaumont-Hamel, to the brook, to the fourth lines of trenches, and had announced their success. So the Newfoundlanders were met as soon as they appeared on the ridge with a converging machine-gun fire, especially from their left, where the north slope across which they marched lay exposed to a southeasterly slope held firmly by the Germans and packed with guns. They did not waver. They hold with a Middlesex regiment the crown of sacrifice in a battle which in that small area seemed almost a defeat.

It was in truth victory, a part of a greater battle triumphantly won at the vital spot. The news from Montauban was the reward, and these men had done as much to win it as the troops, both British and French, who were taking prisoners by the thousand from the German trenches and dugouts above and below the Somme.

The field of this great battle is cut in half by the Ancre. The Ulsters, who were astride the river, divided success from failure. They themselves won ground at Thièpval - though most of it was lost later - and so shared in both fortunes. They were for a while the pivot or hinge of the advance, swinging a little themselves.

But the story of the southern battle is best begun from the southern end. The narrative flows most logically from the capture of Montauban. There our trenches faced the German along a ridge bare of everything except the flowers of such gorgeous weeds as the poppy, cornflower, charlock, and scabious. After the battle these still decorated our abandoned line, but not the German, stretching more than a hundred yards higher up the slope. The contrast was abrupt. The enemy's line had lost all shape and become a chaos of pits and piles and ridges, the most notable tribute to our heavy artillery fire that any soldier had seen. When I wandered over the whole area not long after the battle, some few dugouts remained whole in the first line, but everything in the next line was quite obliterated and the whole was as brown as if just ploughed.

Here two brigades recently recruited from Lancashire towns, especially Manchester, faced some very stalwart Bavarian troops. The attacking part of these two brigades was over the first German line at 7.32 A.M. on Saturday morning, "two minutes after the pistol sounded" Smoke clouds served them well over one section, and when they reached the trenches, in force little diminished, many Bavarians, tired and cowed by shell fire, surrendered. We were helped by the proverbial precision of the French 75's, exploding as close in front of our men as if the gunners were on the spot and not two to three miles away. We captured, among much other material (much of which I saw as it was being collected), three fieldguns, four machine-guns, and three Minenwerfer.

The soldierly qualities of the men were illustrated as much in the defence as the attacks. The trenches they fortified by Montauban had been so ploughed and harrowed by our artillery that they were little or no protection. But the work of consolidation went so quickly that an hour or two later they were able to throw back with terrible losses to the enemy and small to themselves the most determined counter-attack delivered by the Germans at any part of the field. The troops on their left (held up by machine-gun fire from a redoubt nicknamed the "Warren" and less well served with smoke) went more slowly. But they went surely and were very well led by their officers. The East Surreys made a famous charge, and were able to direct other troops round the worst of the machine gun fire.

By steady and persistent fighting the worst danger-spot was passed; the supporting troops, who advanced rather to the right of their original line, filtered down to the left; and so, though some Germans were left behind, they took and fortified a good line running from Montauban westwards to an orchard and beyond it. The "Warren" was finally ferreted out and some eight hundred prisoners captured. On the victory here the successes of the following days, weeks, and months were founded.

The advance at Montauban was the deepest. The ground won here sloped to a narrower band tapering towards Mametz, a village down the slope, separated by a narrow valley from Fricourt. The German trenches were taken at the gallop all along this line, but the village and trenches beside it made a redoubtable fort, not much the less strong for being a mass of ruins almost indistinguishable.

Gordons and Devons especially distinguished themselves by charging through a tornado of machine-gun fire from gunners who had arisen from impermeable dugouts. In spite of heavy losses and the consequent confusion (after the fighting many a north-countryman and south-countryman lay each in the line of the other's front, a pitiful record of the day), both regiments went straight through, bombed the machine-gunners to death, held the line, and later, by swinging forward their left up the valley, completely mastered the village.

Trenches were soon pushed out beyond it and preparations made for the final *coup* - the capture of the Fricourt salient. Fricourt village, the strongest place in the line, was left to the enemy, un-attacked. On the other side of it an amazing fight was fought. This German promontory of Fricourt, flanking the right of the advance, was full of undestroyed machine guns (I found the very emplacements two days later), and before the end of the day it was given rather a wider berth than was at first intended. But, in face of every menace, up the great bare regular hill in front of them the troops, most of them English, struggled so persistently that at the end of the day they reached the landmark at the top, sent up a signal that they were in Crucifix Trench, under the conspicuous Calvary and line of trees that fringe the slope.

The difficulties were of every sort. A message had reached them that the division on the left had won all along the line, but the news was premature. The advance was an advance only of small groups who could not make good the ground till later. So this division was running a double gauntlet between walls of enemies. Machine-guns fired from right flank and left flank, sweeping all lateral roads clean. Our officers were picked off by snipers, who stood beside each enemy's machine-gunner. Crucifix Trench, which had been knocked to pieces by our guns, gave poor shelter and was bombarded heavily from ten to twelve on Saturday night by the enemy. But our miners, including the

Durham Light Infantry, fought a great fight, and the men did more than hold firm. They made sallies and pushed out little efforts everywhere, especially in the small woods.

I saw a score of these efforts from the opposite hill during the next two days. This new army division - who for no fault of their own had partially failed in a previous battle - began an advance which, lasted without intermission for three days and three nights. They fought up the hill and over the crest, always advancing but never gaining the length of a cricket pitch without close and bitter opposition.

The next day you could tell by the bodies lying on the field just where the machine-guns had mown a swathe, and what troops - at the point all were English county troops - had "faced the music" nevertheless. They had crossed a sunken road, exactly as a driven rabbit would cross a ride, with expert shots on either side. Some were left in the road, but some got over.

The advance never ceased, in spite of all, till the full objective was attained, the end reached, the aim won after seventy hours. And it was all intelligent righting, never blind. Once when they were checked, lighter trench mortars, which did admirable work throughout, were hurried forward, the artillery were informed, and a flanking piece of trench cleared by bombs. Then the advance went on as before.

Scores of individual feats of daring were recorded.

A machine-gunner (who had made one of a small party feeling their way into Birch Tree Wood towards the right) found himself in the sequel all alone, forced to hide for the whole night in a shell hole, while the wood was being blown to pieces. I had seen that very bombardment from the opposite hill by our artillery. Incidentally he killed one German officer who had painfully raised himself on his haunches to shoot one of our wounded.

In front of Crucifix Trench, to the left, the enemy made repeated bombing attacks from a redoubt. In reply, a wounded officer and a handful of men even made an effort to take this hornets' nest themselves. It was not finally captured until the third night, but in it there surrendered 700 prisoners; 400 more were taken in Crucifix Trench. Two other woods, where German machine-guns had successfully hidden, were occupied earlier.

In the end, after two days of bulldog righting scarcely surpassed in the war, the division joined hands with troops advancing through and behind Fricourt. The German line, the strongest fortifications ever elaborated on the field, was broken, and a mile and more of land behind it carried and made strong.

There remains the battle of two divisions opposite Boiselle and a part of Thièpval. Opposite Boiselle an enormous mine was blown, the largest as yet seen. It is now a cemetery, and men are buried in the chalk sides just as they fell. Past this crater the charge went welL It was here that the Tynesiders, altogether irresistible, dashed straight through to Contalmaison, where we found some few of the wounded six days later. But at no part in the line was the German device of bending to the storm and rising when the blast was over quite so deadly. The first waves went clean through, and messages of their success were sent off. But the enemy rose quickly and in great numbers behind them from the cellar trenches. Some machine-guns were directed at the backs of the men who had passed, some at the later waves as they advanced. In the sequel the leaders were quite cut off and the rest stopped. The first attack had failed; but it was repeated with as fine determination as any troops showed, and in spite of the set-back the village was won the next day and an awkward position made good.

Yet harder work and not less deadly befell the troops opposite Ovillers and part of Thièpval. They faced a dominant position, held by picked troops who had remained constant to fortresses they regarded with personal pride. Between our attacking trenches and the German was a very wide and very open space on an up-slope, obnoxious to direct and enfilading fire. The men to whom this task was given had fought with conspicuous determination at the Hohenzollern Redoubt and other hot centres of struggle; and here they made a new reputation. The punishment received as they delivered the assault across this unprotected front affected their determination as little as a breath of contrary wind. The impossibility of reinforcing the storming party with either men or munitions compelled retreat at the end of the day; but the Leipsic Redoubt, a corner-stone of the German defence, remained in our hands, and its possession opened the path to those three brilliant assaults that won us Thièpval two months later.

No battle, no period of warfare in our annals proved the doggedness of British will in more stubborn fashion than the struggle of the divisions fighting between Fricourt and the Ancre. Each won its way by inches, almost without artillery aid. The infantry were so close to the enemy, often in so confused a shape that no cannon of longer range than a trench mortar could be used. The most persistent, most daring, most intelligent men won by virtue of their human quality. In the days that followed, the whole of Ovillers and the barrens round and about it were won by sheer grit, what the German philosophers call the will to conquer. If that will is the hall-mark of the superman, then our civilian soldiers are more than human. Throughout this neighbourhood our county troops - Wilts, Warwicks, Gloucesters, Surreys, Kents, Sussex, Hertfordshires, and a number beside - played as great a part as the Australians who took up the torch at Pozières or the Middlesex in the final attack at Thièpval. And to say that is to say as much as can be said of any of the stuff of the fighting soldier.

Perhaps it gives a wrong impression to treat the attack on 1st July as a separate event, but it will always remain a day of days in our history. Waterloo is an episode compared with it. The New Army then tried its strength, stormed a position often attacked and thought impregnable, a position held by troops trained for the dominance of the world and equipped with all the death dealing weapons that a devilish science could invent or a devilish desire multiply.

Only those who were in France at the time and among the civil population can understand the effect of the battle on public opinion. It was a pity that wholly fantastic stories of British losses spread abroad, to be afterwards reported in German wireless messages to neutral countries. But these were an after growth. The courage, the calmness, the cheerfulness of the British soldier was the theme of France. Some said it was "magnificent, but not war"; but this view steadily faded before the solid success of the following months; and ever after from that day the British soldier was looked upon as a being who could smile in the face of death with a quiet faith stronger than the hope of glory or the passion of hate.

The day must remain cardinal in our annals for every reason. For the first time in history the British nation, as a force embracing and annulling the old little gallant army, tried its 'prentice strength in a great battle; and it fleshed its teeth against the greatest enemy in the world, an enemy who for years had willed war, had harnessed the passive flesh and blood of its manhood, not less than the engines of its science, to the work of destroying its neighbours and plundering their country.

As the latest move in this campaign of dominance, begun forty years ago and more, it had for tressed this veteran army in more than Cretan labyrinths of earth, on the slopes and crests of hills behind which roared the great engines that were to cooperate with the lesser devilries of chemistry and mechanics, to the obliteration of the peace and power of France and Britain and their allies.

The battle that opened in the mist of the summer morning was a thing by itself; yet also part of a sequence. It was the sequel to near two years of inordinate struggle, and it lasted at high pressure for five months, through the heats of summer and the rains and mists of autumn, lulling only when in the dark days of winter the soaked earth refused to part with its moisture; and fighting became a crude struggle with mud and bodily weariness. We may take as its end the achievement of its first purpose - the capture of Beaumont Hamel on 14th November, rounding off the possession of the twin bastions of Thièpval, just across the Ancre, and the high land, about the little hamlet of Ginchy, on our southern and right wing.

CHAPTER V
ON THE BATTLE-FIELD

A GREAT CHALK hill, now mangled and overgrown out of all likeness to cultivated land, runs behind the Peronne road, which may be taken as the base of our great advance. For two years no one has been able to show a head there without risk of losing it. You moved only in deep and winding trenches, and if you looked through a slit in the parapet you were at pains to have no light behind when you withdrew the sand-bag curtain from the crevice. Such underground life was of the atmosphere of the whole war. The coming of a time when men should prefer the open to the tunnel was a prospect scarcely present to the imagination. When the change came it was difficult to grasp its reality. "Can this be true?" we asked. It was so true that on 2nd July I picnicked, strolled, stood tiptoe on mounds within full sight of the fighting and ran no risk.

Did ever man watch modern battle in such tranquillity? I felt like the figures in the old illustrations of Froissart where perspective drawing was not in fashion and men stood winding crossbows within arm's length of a drawn long-bow. Yet the battle just across the valley was as bloody and bitter as any in history, and in every way more full of terror.

Old soldiers always used to say of this war that South Africa was a picnic to it. To us out of the hurly-burly the conditions were picnic conditions. It was high treason to the God of War so to watch his battle.

The road runs in the valley below, passing the village of Fricourt, which was soon to become almost a trippers' haunt. On the farther slope the battle raged, visible in palpable detail from the hither ridge, my vantage-point. Here the ground, neglected these two years by cultivators, was extravagantly brilliant with poppies, cornflowers, corn-cockles, scabious (the blue and the purple), charlock, wild geraniums, bladder campion, thistles, and many precious little flowers, including gentians. All the trenches made brilliant lines of yellow and red, where the poppy and charlock weeds had fastened on parapet and parados.

Here you could wander where you would in the open, running no risk except for a few spent machine-gun bullets from the other hill and perhaps a dropping bullet from a fighting or practising airman. Both were heard.

The whine and whirring of the shells overhead destroyed the extravagant peacefulness; but even these seemed to encourage nature to assert itself. In every battle that I watched from this field the larks sang to distraction from an hour before dawn, and generally a quail trilled in the undergrowth. As for the hawks, they curvetted everywhere.

To feel and realize the nature of the fight called for an effort of conscious will, though the movement was visible enough and even particular. I saw men's arms bowling bombs, and groups of surrendering enemy were so big as to be unmistakable with the naked eye. The observer saw a drama moving beyond imagination, but a drama without words, without a key to the entrances and exits, the comings and goings, the meetings and partings. In the course of the Somme battle I have watched, as others have watched, a succession of episodes compact of human tragedy, of death and of triumph over death, but then, and for all time, vague as the stuff of dreams. On that 2nd day of July, standing among the flowers, I saw hour after hour the battle move up the opposite slope past Fricourt, towards a drop curtain of smoke pillars and under a canopy of intolerable tumult. Little groups of prisoners scuttling back furtively gave news of advance and victory; but victory without definition, without nicely pencilled precision or satisfied curiosity. You were forced to guess at the plot, though certain acts or parts and all the scenes were clear enough.

We were attacking beyond all question. The double German barrage was as obvious as the blue sky. Our remoter barrier had the conspicuousness of an eruption. But what were those eight men meaning to do? What was their part in the plot? What was their fate? They left the trench. Quite soon, just as they passed a patch of chalky soil, they lay down. They remained lying down, for an hour, for two hours. Some one thought one of them moved. Some one thought not. Shells fell here and there in front of them, but not mortally near. Were they told to lie and wait till the others came up, till a machine-gun was silenced? or were they already beyond orders, immortally silent?

The spectators will never know, and history will only say that the plot came to a proper, a successful *dénouement*. But on the brain, on the mind's eye of some observers that picture of the eight men who lay down beyond the bump of muddy chalk will remain stereotyped, quite indestructible, the fabric of an unforgotten mystery.

For many days the panorama of battle, though not its living features, was visible from this hill; and the scene changed strangely with the weather and the nature of the fighting. A week later one stopped there to observe the spectacle of our bombardment of the second German line. On Sunday, the 9th of July, so clear was the air after its washing by the thunder rain that the whole battlefield, as seen from those almost Olympian thrones on it and about it, seemed to have changed its scale. It was under a magnifying glass.

In the valley and up the slope a delta of trenches was etched out, each delta separated from the next by a great fort or dam: Montauban, Mametz, Fricourt, La Boillsee - the whole a maze, labyrinthine, Dædalian. Critics talk of crossing one, two, three, four German trenches. We crossed fifty, running in as many directions as the diagram of a snow crystal.

There are short, fat bunches of trenches; longlegged, vagrant trenches, canal-like trenches, which some foul machine-gun could rake from a forgotten village ruin a kilometre away. There are tight, narrow trenches, and chambered trenches; trenches in the open; trenches that play hide-and-seek through cellars or among the roots of trees. Trenches run horizontally, vertically, diagonally to the front, boxing the compass and confounding geometry.

This system, formed slowly as a real delta is formed, we had taken root and branch over an 8 miles' front, without reckoning minor gains to the north and the spacious French gains to the south. The atmosphere spaced out the marvel of the victory as well as the features of the battle-field.

In occasional visits to the front during the years of stagnancy we had approached the top of this Observation Hill without seeing it. It was difficult enough to find a point where you could look into the valley. All this was changed; for a week and more I almost lived - always in the open - on this hill, night and day. Once a poor padre, walking in apparent security some fifty yards in front of me, was hit by a shell. Once, at a much later date, a visitor from England was sent helter-skelter into a dugout, where he dived into a group of Scotchmen, by the near explosion of the first of a series of shells. Occasionally a few odd shells went whining by; but the place in general was as free from danger, or the sense of danger, as a place could be. An artillery observer or two sat on camp stools and fixed their glasses on tripods, aligning them day after day on ever-lengthening and more distant targets. All day the horizon smoked with constant pillars where our batteries were directed; and fitfully at intervals German shells barking, like sulky mastiffs, would crowd to this spot or that. At one time they would avenue the approaches to Contalmaison, while our horses, brave as men, went through without shirking, though never without nerves. They too had seen the bodies of their predecessors and the remnants of limbers and lorries dragged off the fairway to make room for the unceasing traffic.

Up this ridge some of us used to stumble at night, tripping over wires, skirting trenches, sheltering in rain under old gun emplacements, wading through woods of thistles, and as the time went out passing through small encampments and hearing the ring of a sentry's challenge. For the hill was as wonderful a vantage point at night as at day. I went there to sleep in the open, but the view banished sleep. The spectacle was never stale nor the effect the same, and often one awaited some great morning attack, and was alert to hear the sudden thunder of its announcement. The night signals, white and green and red, shot up continuously at certain places. These we had marked down on the map, duly aligned, and could tell just at what point along what trenches the enemy or ourselves were growing nervous of a night attack.

The strangeness of these lights is their seeming nearness. One of the more intensely bright German star-shells - they are hardly less visible by

76

day than night - would seem to fall into the thistles a few hundred yards down the slope; and you wondered that it did not light up the faces of your companions, though you knew it was one of the continuous galaxy by which the Germans hoped to anticipate our unceasing attack along their trenches at Ovillers and Boiselle, two and three miles away.

Such scenes had grown curiously familiar and almost commonplace to me after a fortnight's fighting, but no single night remains so vivid as the eve of our great attack on 14th July. I had known the preparations for the attack, which was of peculiar difficulty. We were to assault the German trenches, take the villages of Bazentin and Longueval, as well as the woods alongside them, in a night venture more complicated than had ever been attempted even in manoeuvres. The day before, one of the chief generals concerned had penetrated into No Man's Land (with a cavalry officer, who accompanied him "for fun," as he told us) to see with his own eyes whether the wire had been properly cut. As I waited on the hill for the coming of the zero hour of 3.30 in the morning, I could imagine the new troops of his division who were to make the first charge creeping forward into No Man's Land and massing in the trenches; and so real was the picture on the mind's eye that dim lumps of earth close in front took on the semblance of crouching men, and the still slope below was as full of fighting men as the real battle scene in Caterpillar valley. A day of battle doubles sensation and vitalizes movement. And we had all been waiting, listening, watching, till every sense was at the pitch of alertness, except the sense of hearing, which was utterly dulled by the continuous dinning of the guns.

Yet how old and familiar everything was: old and familiar in this strange war the larks that long before dawn persisted in singing through the gunthunder as if they had "a faculty for storm and turbulence"; the whistling quail in the weedflowers; the aeroplanes that shot in the half-dark straight as a bullet for the battle; and after dawn the ugly bulbous balloons swaying in the wind.

Nevertheless, excitement made all new.

In the very summit of the bombardment, just before the attacking moment, for which one waited watch in hand, I looked vaguely at the obscurity of a familiar landscape, when mysteriously out of the enchantment of the twilight there stood out (almost stepped out of the gloom) the rank of well-known places in a new guise: the skeleton of Contalmaison, the corpse of Fricourt, the pyre of the wood. A cessation of gun-fire would have startled one less.

It was curious to observe how long the battle lights of the armies continue to outface the growing daylight. The signals sent up by ourselves and by the enemy were so many and so mingled as to confuse the very elect. A fire lit by our guns in Longueval was mistaken for the redness of sunrise; and a novel signal, made with a rush of red fire like a Bessemer furnace, was thought to be a colossal shell burst behind the trees. Even after daybreak clouds still threw back the cannon flashes and Germans made sight more certain by showers of Verey lights.

However close you are to the fighting, unless you are a very part of it, a sense of unreality envelops the scene. You catch the turbid glimpses, as of a formless moon, half revealed and half concealed by a drift of stormy wrack. From this half limbo of unsatisfied wonder an irresistible compulsion drives one to the very place where fighting has been. Under such attraction some of us on 3rd July descended from the flowery slope into the valley of the shadow, past the guns, across the road, and into the village and wood of Fricourt. You could see there nothing of the battle, though it raged half a mile or less in front and now and then a great shell re-ploughed the soil or re-ruined the waste of houses. There in the valley nothing was indistinct, nothing dimly glorious. The pomp of war was immobilized in the ruin of its own creation. The dead lay where they fell beside the dead houses, and what movement there was, was the movement of the stretcher-bearers.

A glorious division had charged the trenches running south from the village of Mametz. One group of Gordons and Devons caught by a machine gun - which the few survivors destroyed - lay in all the attitudes and abandonment of death, one single figure half propped up by the bayonet which had run into the ground. Along with them, dead as they, lay their little mascot terrier, "true to death" as in the old epitaph. He was not humble enough to escape the swing of the scythe, the serried sweep of machine-gun bullets, which the Germans delight to aim low, to spray as a waterhose sprays, that the live may fall, and the wounded be killed, and the dying exterminated. But a battle-field after victory is robbed of some of its sting. The very attitudes of the dead, fallen eagerly forward, have a look of expectant hope. You would say that they died with the light of victory in their eyes. These men by Mametz went a quarter of a mile in the open, starting from trenches farther back than they had meant. Germans from the woody slope opposite had marked the place of the assaulting trench, and filled it in with 5.9 shells. Indeed, firing at this place became a habit. Though you could walk in comfort anywhere else, it was always "unhealthy" just there where the trench had been destroyed below the village.

The oppression of a battle is the sight of your own dead; but on a field of victory such as this, the shrinking muddle of the German dead lying in the ditches or just outside emplacements and dugouts, as they began to flee, was more deeply touched with the horror of war. If our men were as signposts on the road to victory, these men, more distinctly still, pointed the way to fear and defeat.

A battle-field not yet swept of its debris - and this will take years to sweep - is not a place visited for pleasure, but at least it serves for tribute to the irrepressible gallantry and endurance of soldiers. On the bright, pleasant Sunday morning succeeding the opening of the battle, the wounded were still being salved, and it was not yet time to attend to the dead. As I crossed the fields beyond the Peronne road on the way to Mametz, the stretcher bearers passed me in successive groups, bearing yesterday's wounded, some British, some German.

What the Germans had gone through was written on every yard of the captured ground. Their trench *de luxe* on the near side of Mametz village was virtually filled in by our shell-fire. Many of the dugouts were still completely blocked. Into others, where the doorways were clear, our stretcher bearers descended by flights of twenty and twenty five steps, to find at the bottom heaps of dead, and among them here and there a few still breathing.

It was a task of both delicacy and strength to rescue these wounded from the dead, to lift them up the broken and narrowed stairway, and carry them, often without recourse to a trench, back to the dressing-station. But the men attended to these half-buried creatures as if they had been friends; and it would need a more than stony heart not to be glad to watch at close quarters the men at their life-saving work and to see that the spirit of that Sunday morning - or native kindness - was strong on them to make no distinction between friend and enemy. And the Germans were grateful. "They are very kind," was the general refrain; and when a man who has lain out twenty four hours has the force to say such a thing, he means what he says.

The patrol of the stretcher-bearers, the absorbing business of saving life and diminishing pain, lends some humanity to the after-day of battle. You forget the dead in the living; just as the stretcher bearers themselves, even in the hottest parts of the fight, will forget shells and bullets when once they have found their wounded man and begun to place him on the stretcher. Though they were trembling and livid with fear before, from that moment the sting of the nervousness, the sense of brutality in the scene leaves them. They too are no longer fighting in cold blood.

A battle-field is more forbidding on the third day than the first or second - or so it seemed to me. My memory of 2nd July near Mametz is of lifesavers at work. My memory of Fricourt wood and village on 3rd July is of a violated graveyard; and the sense of all subsequent fields, save one, was the same. Wherever a man went in the wake of battle, he stumbled over a country shaken by more than an earthquake in a land of extinct civilizations - past old battery positions, like the halls or gateways of departed mansions, tangles of wire, and blind trenches; shell holes, brown and new, or gorgeous as sunken gardens, with thyme and forget-me-nots and poppies; new and hidden batteries that hit and punched you unaware with an intolerable blast; skeletons of horses and horses dead since yesterday; trees all wrenched and torn and pitted by fire; buildings, separate or in groups, with never a room or corner fit for anything but road making.

When through such a country on the morning of 3rd July I walked down the slope to Fricourt, the German guns by some miracle were almost silent. The once neat village lying snug and prosperous at the foot of the protective wood might have been shattered in an exhausted earthquake. The living enemy gave no sign; and as you approached you saw no dead: the dead are always modest, lying as obscure as they may. But the battle-field was still unswept, as presently each step disclosed; and I was conscious of feeling a great relief when the first body was a German, a victim of the gallant East Yorkshireman who lay beyond.

Every yard of the village was strewn with the debris of ordinary life as well as of war. So one would expect of "homes" - save the mark! - cosily inhabited for a year or more. The blankets were half thrown back from the beds. Beer-bottles, cigarette tins, toilet things lay there alongside trenching tools, "hair-brush" grenades, - unbroached, like the beer-bottles, - many bandoliers full of cartridges, and here and there little works of art carved by the householder in his spare moments.

In some dugouts candles were still burning. One could have carried away tons, wagon-loads of mementoes if one's principal idea - I speak for myself - was not to forget the scene as soon as might be. The *memento mori* is not an adorable souvenir.

It is useless at this date in a war of necessary iconoclasm to describe a ruined village, even if it is hot with the horror of battle. But here I saw one pregnant symbol which might serve for a painter of the madness of war. A single cultivator or shallow plough remained untouched among the dust and rubble. I suppose it had stood in the yard of the farmer's house; but now street and house and yard were quite indistinguishable, except where a trench revealed foundations. I mistook a revolving corn grinder for an engine of war, and found a ploughshare used in the defence of a dugout. Yet the summit of destruction is still incomplete. In spite of the upheaval of bricks and mortar and the eruption of earth from under the very foundations of the houses, many dugouts and machine-gun emplacements were nevertheless undamaged.

It was unpleasant and ghoul-like, and yet in some sort exciting, to creep down the pinched stairways of the deeper dugouts. You were wise to avoid kicking the many "hair-brush" grenades left unused; and once I saw one of our Mills bombs. There was always a feeling that you might come suddenly upon an inmate, dead or alive; and some were found even later than this crouching frightened into corners, afraid either to fight or surrender.

As I crept up again into the trench from one of these lairs, I heard the machine-guns rattle out in front with some extra intensity. It was, I think, the moment when the final attack was pushed home along "Railway Alley" and in "Shelter Wood," just over the brow beyond Fricourt. The noise was almost a relief. The village was not a wholesome place to stay in long, and I had no desire to imitate the manner of Marius in the ruins of Carthage. Besides, for the purpose of seeing the progress of the battle, it was much better to be on the hill, where the flowers grew and the action was visible.

A battle-ground in the open country is less oppressive. One of the following days I spent some hours over the stretch of country in front of Montauban, where the Manchester troops had routed the Bavarians. The causes of victory, the nature of the victory, the experiences of the two forces on the previous day, were so printed that the mind was alert to read the story and could forget for moments the stagnant disgust belonging to a field of destruction.

The scene along this complicated system of German ditches and caves in front of Montauban is as difficult to convey in words as the sensation aroused in investigating it. Standing on a mound of earth thrown up by a 12-inch shell, I could see one brilliant line of green and red and yellow stretching indefinitely along the ridge. This was composed of the grass and poppies and charlock growing on the parapet of what was our front-line trench till 1st July. Fifty to a hundred yards beyond it stretched a belt of earth, quite 150 yards broad, completely weeded of all vegetation whatever. It consisted wholly of brown and white pits and circular ridges cutting one another in fantastic patterns. This was the ex-German system of front trenches with their intervening spaces. You can still trace the trenches - the biggest is Breslau Avenue - if you move carefully and watch closely, but that is all that remains of the original pattern.

I found one or two dugouts that I could crawl into, but one does not crawl twice into a grave if one is not forced - even an enemy's grave; so I left all but the first alone. Most of the caves had openings about the size of a fox's earth or a rat's hole. Some were clean vanished, either under a mound or in the embrace of a rival pit - a pit sometimes 18 feet deep and 26 feet across. One cavern had still the lintel of the door intact, and on it was written in chalk, *"Zum Thai der Liebe"* ("At the Sign of Love Valley!"). An iron pipe chimney coming from a miniature grate, with a tin of soup hung by wire over it, stuck out from another. But the force of destruction could hardly go farther. No officer, British or French, had ever seen completer ruin.

The appalling work of battle-field salvage was going busily on; and the stacks of rifles, of cartridges and cases, of woollen fabric were rising only less quickly than shocks in a new corn-field. This was one event. In another village close to the fighting a most reverent service for a hundred of our dead laid out on the earth was being held by three padres of different denominations. But in those dugouts I had avoided were scores of men whose bodies no man will ever find, unless it be the ploughman or the architect in the days of peace, still too distant to seem real.

Wherever we crossed the old German front line, the battle-field was the strangest and thorniest in history. Beaumont-Hamel out-did even Fricourt and Montauban. Indeed the men who four months later stormed the positions north of the Ancre and along it might have been advancing over roofs in a street fight. Underneath them were rooms upon rooms containing hidden and unsuspected groups, and down in the street -trenches below - some nearly empty, some crowded - the enemy lifted their hands and shouted for mercy or occasionally fired into the air.

Such battle-fields remain unsearched or unplumbed. Pockets of men, dumps of stores, reserves of weapons lie hidden here, there, and everywhere. The scale of the hiding-places is on the scale of a town of many streets and well-cellared houses. The trenches themselves are as tangled as the pattern of a quick-set hedge in winter, and the maze of crooked lines, interspersed with dugout holes, extends to a breadth of over a mile. A section of ground cut through Oxford Street would hardly be more intricate.

The crowning marvel of the German defence was revealed on 13th November on the south bank of the Ancre. If you slip along the river road you come to an opening about 7 feet high in the clay cliff, and when you have penetrated into the secret place you find a new world - a Monte Cristo world. Even the guns, which thunder to madness outside, are blurred to a murmur; indeed, are often wholly inaudible. A sickly reek pervades the place - not the reek of dead bodies, though a few wounded men from the battle, vainly seeking shelter here, lie where they have fallen in the passages. Meat and bread perhaps have mouldered in the stores, and the volatile dust of the fungus blends with the pungent dankness of the clay.

But those who first entered this cavern had no other thoughts than curiosity or apprehension. They walked into the unknown, on and on, round one traverse after another, until the broad corridor - 7 feet high and as much in breadth - was cut by another of like sort leading right and left. The leg of this T-shaped avenue is about 300 yards, and the arms - not yet fully explored - are at least 200. Double bedrooms and chambers of various sizes lead off from the corridor. Some are papered; all may be lit by electricity, and the upholstery is sufficient. Panelling is frequent. How many men could barrack here I do not know; but over 400 enemy soldiers took refuge during the attack and filed out meekly after it was over. Perhaps the place was used as much for a storehouse as a barracks; and we know that quantities of machine-guns and other trench weapons were kept there.

A country-side strewn with dead and with wreckage of all that had value and claimed affection should kill any vestige of feelings for the glory of war. One dead horse will do that. Crossing Fricourt from this side to that, I had felt that I should always see war in terms of the gallant East Yorkshiremen, who lay dead on the north, and the Gordons, Devons, and Manchesters, who lay on the south; but battle-fields were to succeed battlefields day after day, for weeks, for months; and at the end one field was to condense the qualities of all the rest.

On 1st July opposite Beaumont-Hamel, the Newfoundland regiment lost all its officers and nearly three-quarters of its men who went into action. Nearly two years before that was fought, the village was a graveyard, decorated by the German occupants with a grand monument to those who had fallen. At intervals during all this interval, the ground had been pounded, and after every artillery attack the wire had been restored and even increased. So thick it was and close and wide, it looked from the O.P on our side like a broad swathe of newly ploughed land, running all straight and broad, across the edge of the hill. Finally so many of our shells flocked to this spot that the wire, some of it as thick as your little finger, was cut up into short lengths, twisted into fantastic curves, buried, half buried, tossed loose on the surface, till it seemed a part of the soil.

Then, a full nineteen weeks after the first failure, our naval and Scottish troops turned the field of defeat into a field of victory. Again, as at Fricourt, you could infer the victory, particularize the courage, and read, as in a history book, the writing embossed over these gentle undulations of ground leading along the river to Beaucourt. A soldier lay at one spot tightly gripping a German with both hands, the two joined in this last embrace of hate, just as they fell, both, it is probable, shot by a German machine-gun.

For hereabouts the machine-gun was very busy. You could trace the fell course of its discharge by many signs, to which the world would wish to shut his eyes. And yet no. Every one who has walked across the field of battle - and this field perhaps above all others - comes away with an admiration that is indeed reverence for the men who slowly, steadfastly walked that autumn morning one hundred yards after another over fields poisonous with the enemy's devices. When need was they gripped the enemy hand to hand, or they marched without wavering across the evil stream of bullets, or they jumped, sometimes into, sometimes over, trenches thorny with well-armed enemy and volcanic with bombs.

Wire caught and tripped them and tangled them as they stumbled on. It was cut and tumbled everywhere by artillery work of the highest accuracy; but wire, especially German wire, is indestructible as material, and no acres along the front have been so roofed with it. It was like vines in a great vineyard, but vines planted broadcast. Men were shot as they disentangled themselves, coolly as you would dislodge a bramble, and if a wounded man who had already fallen attempted to shift his position he was a dead man; for in all the fighting in this area since 1st July the Germans by deliberate policy have watered the ground with bullets after an attack, and have appointed special snipers to fire at any moving object.

In the gloom and fog of that autumn morning the attack somewhat lost evenness and cohesion - or so the writing suggests - and the groups missed the encouragement of an even charge when every man has companions to follow and feels himself part of a machine. In this advance one group after another relied wholly on itself; and its reliance was not misplaced. Every man, every little assembly of men, went forward, in spite of a hundred barriers that would have plausibly held up platoons or battalions less game than these. They were out to win their spurs. He who runs might read the story - yesterday. To-morrow the characters will have faded: "The finger rubs out the picture." After a famous victory such as this every soldier in the region is too busy with work and with the living to heed the dead. They lie on the field of their fame, as they fell, for a day, it may be for several days. Then - and soon for a field of battle - with quick care and stern reverence the last rites are paid, and the field is dressed in the desolation only of material things: coils of thorny wire, bits of clothing, equipment, torn masks, and broken weapons, and a shattered soil. Only in the caves in the trenches will the sterner ordeal await the loiterer and "the cleaner" on the battle-field.

We have had many great fights; none finer than this. It was heroic in every turn and phase. And the heroism was nowhere vain. Everywhere it won its end, yes, and more than its end. Nor was its cost beyond measure as figures go. It is only that every fibre of feeling is touched to see one good man fallen before he reached the end.

When the fight was over an astonishing silence brooded over the field. The enemy was not using his artillery to any great extent. The scene of quietude at Fricourt on 3rd July, when we were fighting just beyond, was repeated. Both spectacles quite stripped war of any glamour or excitement, though none so stirred admiration for the glory of the British infantry soldier.

Even as he lies on the field he looks more quietly faithful, more simply steadfast than others, as if he had taken care while he died that there should be no parade in his bearing, no heroics in his posture. To see him there was to swear an immortal oath that his sacrifice should not fail of its end - the freedom of his children from the threat of war and the unstained liberty of his nation.

CHAPTER VI
AN EARLIER FIELD

A BATTLE-FIELD, which nature takes instant pains to hide and man as much labour to remember, may be a more moving scene when the time is calm and daily life resumed than ever it was in the noise and heat of the fighting.

But on the Somme even nature has had little chance to relieve the position, so harassed is the field with the coming and going of war and continued shelling. And no inhabitants have yet returned, as they would, whatever the danger, if there were a room or a barn to hold them. How often, traipsing over these unlovely surfaces between Fricourt and High Wood I have thought of the first battle-field that ever I saw in this war. The date of the battle was not three weeks past; and yet nature, with man's assistance, had quite restored the native charm of fields and woods and inhabited houses. The war already seemed a vague mingling of

> *"Old, unhappy, far-off things*
> *And battles long ago."*

This was in October 1914, in the days when the war moved and battles were fought before the eyes of civilians. The contrast is a help to the realization of the outer desolation of the places where war has stayed; and it is a real obligation for the people of inviolate England to feel as well as know what a battle means in itself and in the eyes of the unhappy country people whose village is invaded.

The beautiful village of Montreuil, tucked neatly into its narrow valley, is almost a little town. It has a tiny factory of embroidery and three inns. I reached the spot as it was growing dusk and endeavoured to get lodging at one of the "hotels." But I failed. "The Germans have stolen everything: our sheets, our blankets, our tablecloths, our napkins, our clothes, our knives and forks, even our clocks." As I walked up the street after the last failure I met the postmaster, and we began to talk. Within a few minutes a circle of villagers surrounded us. "He is English," some one had said, and the word went round with mysterious speed. If anyone wishes to face the difficult task of accepting deep and open gratitude let him go to any of the French villages between the Marne and the Aisne from which the British chased the Germans.

"Oh, but they are fine soldiers."

"And how quick they march."

"And they shoot - oh, it is a marvel."

"What misery it was till the English came and saved us. Oh, the brave soldiers."

There was a slight pause in the chorus. Then a woman said: "We have buried some on the hill"; and her daughter: "And we take flowers every day. Yes, monsieur, every day; fresh flowers from the gardens and the fields" Then the postmaster hailed a young man who was to join the colours in three days and bade him guide me up the hill. We passed between the houses, up an open drive, deeply trenched by the Germans on one bank; and so to the top of the hill. There was a cart at one side of the lane, and the young man, who seemed suddenly awkward and nervous and silent, took off his cap. We were standing close by the soldiers' grave, which the cart and the dusk had concealed from me. A comely rustic cross marked the head, and other fagoted crosses the surface. Between them were dahlias and daisies and even roses from the village gardens, and a tight-knit bunch, such as children make, of blue succory and other wild flowers. In a square about the grave and at some yards' distance was cut a neat trench, and on the edge a low rustic fence was begun. The young man replaced his cap, turned round brusquely, and, with a jerk of his hand, said: "We buried the Germans there." Within a few yards of the English grave the ground was sunk and rough, but for the rest undistinguished from the field. There was no mark or ridge even, only the spits of earth, half crumbled as thrown up by the spade. "We shall put a sign later just to show where they were put," said the young man; and we returned to the village, where the night had become almost as dark as the unlit houses.

I spent the night in a hospitable house almost on the battle-field. An English bullet was stuck tight in the bricks of the gate-post, and my host showed me how another bullet had penetrated the sash of his bedroom window, passed between the blankets and counterpane of the bed, making a mark like a caterpillar under the bark, and fallen spent against the opposite wall. But the house was saved by lying in a little hollow on the slope. In the morning we visited the battle-field. It was sufficiently conspicuous, thanks to seven German caissons left on the field; but for the rest nature was covering up the traces with strange completeness and speed. Yet even without a guide we could have reconstructed much of the scene and detected the tactical ingenuity of the German colonel. The ground had been dug in three patterns. A shallow pit of wide dimensions surrounded by a low ridge of earth marked the position of the big guns. Round the circle of earth and outside it were quantities of apples rotting on the ground, and - now withered and battered - the big boughs of fruit trees with which the batteries had been most persuasively masked. The colonel had been too clever to put his guns in the wood which was close by. Instead he had himself made a new orchard. In these days "the woods of Dunsinane" move as a matter of course.

The second pattern or device consisted of deep, narrow holes - exploded wasps' nests - with a steep ridge of earth in front. They had housed the machine-guns. You could detect these holes at a distance and in many parts of the field by reason of the brilliant greenness surrounding them. They had all been cloaked by stooks of ripe grain which had already germinated. These hubs of death and destruction - as it was meant by their makers - had suffered an earth change into the very stuff of peace and life, as if to show in perfect symbol that the man who sows the grain is the master of us all; and beyond him and his work that things sweet and fresh and green, almost before we know it, shall get the better of the short lived evil of wanton madness. The third pattern was the soldiers' trench. As we entered the field I noticed a covey of partridges rise from the unexpected pitch of an abandoned ammunition cart. On inspection it was clear that the caissons too had been covered with sheaves and straw, and the partridges were picking up the relic grain even in the hollows where the ammunition had lain. The field was strewn with several hundred unused shells, spilled and neglected by the fleeing Germans.

Now for the battle itself. The German colonel, who had stayed with my host, had been politeness itself. When once he had stolen the motor, he abstained, like a gentleman, from all petty pillage. At an early hour one Wednesday morning he was suddenly summoned, and his manner became nervous and brusque. He and his brother-officer demanded at once strong black coffee in quantity. They were given it, not in cups, but in the soupbowls always used in this part of France. The men drank off five bowls of this, "till their hearts must have beat like bells," as my hostess said. The colonel left saying, "There will be a battle. It will probably last three days. We shall be back to sleep." A little later the first gun was fired. It raged from 7 A.M. to 4.30 P.M. without much apparent change, except that some British infantry had pushed up from the hill three miles away to some woods flanking the German position. From a slit in the cellar of one of the houses an English aeroplane could be seen passing in baffled circles round and round the scene.

In the afternoon a young man who had crept out to observe saw this aeroplane turn quickly and make straight back to the neighbourhood of the British battery, which had begun to fire rather spasmodically. There was a pause. Then a sudden outbreak, and in ten minutes the battle was over. In two of the circles where the six German guns had been placed, which at last the airman had detected, there was a deep hole made by an exploding shell, right in the middle, a perfect bull's-eye. "Oh, but they shoot well," was no vain compliment. The six guns were abandoned and all the ammunition. The British infantry advanced rapidly, losing some men from the fire of a machine-gun, and a few were wounded by cross-fire from their own flanking bodies. But the battle was over, and our troops came within 400 yards of the Germans, now in full retreat. Sixty-one Germans are buried in one of the many graves and forty-six in another. On the left many prisoners were taken. "The colonel," said my host, "was among the slain. He did not return to sleep."

As I walked away on a journey northwards nearer the sound of the guns which reached the village as a dull boom of little meaning, two peasants - a man and his wife - were manuring and ploughing the field. The plough and horses and man silhouetted against the sky remain a more vivid picture than any war scene of them all.

Nothing of this sort is to be seen over the Somme fields. Once, after the rush forward on 15th September, we reached cultivated fields near Warlencourt, and one charge was delivered through a field of red cabbages. Peasants, men and women, are a brave class. They come very close to the lines where the battle is stagnant. In Belgium many peasants quite disregarded the fighting, and some few were forcibly driven away from work between the two lines, which were separated in many places by cultivated crops.

A delightful story may be told of the effect of the crops on the problems. A brigadier, not too fond of visiting his front trenches, came out one autumn morning after an exceptionally long absence. He entered an observation niche and peered for a long time across No Man's Land. At last, turning round, he said: "The Germans are preparing to attack. Telephone to the artillery." The artillery replied to the message that they would send down their own observer. He proved to be a slow and quiet young man with a pronounced drawl; but one glimpse assured him that the Germans had neither lowered their parapet nor taken away their wire as the brigadier feared; and the message that he sent back over the telephone was this: "Don't worry, battery. It's only that the turnips have grown!"

Nothing that is or might have been a turnip exists on the Somme field, nor any house nor any barn nor any civilian. Even the woods are scarcely recognizable. Just to test the ruin, I walked one day in a bee-line for four long miles across a country once rich in crops and villages. At no spot anywhere could I detect the remnant of any crop. I passed through one large and one small village, and could find no single house or outhouse with any remnant of a roof or presentable wall. Never once in all the journey was I as much as ten yards from a shell hole. Two little woods that I passed possessed no single tree of a natural form. A number were up by the roots, and the floor was strewn with the offal of shells and weapons and bits of tree; and in the midst of each was a single field-gun knocked out of all shape and half smothered with the twisted steel girders and broken concrete blocks that had defended it.

Will the peasants ever again in this generation return to their home-land and work their ploughs?

CHAPTER VII
OVER THE PARAPET

DURING JULY AND August, and until we topped the final ridge, it was an easy thing to reach points from which the charge of our men was visible in detail even to the naked eye. A general who asked some of us to come on the morrow and watch his men "go over," had that day actually faced his own charging troops, so abrupt was the salient. The men charged north-east by east. His watch-place at 1000 yards distance faced northwest by west.

The greatest thing that can be asked of any soldier is to "go over the top" in battle as developed by German skill in mechanical warfare; and nothing is more characteristic of the nature of the British soldier than his humorous discussions of this final test. We take our pleasures sadly - *nous nous amusons trisiement* - perhaps; certainly we take our pains gaily. The heroism of leaping the parapet is laughed into the leapfrog game of "jumping the lid."

On 1st July, 100,000 men went over the top, or the lid; and among them all was no straggler. "There were no stragglers," said every general, every officer; and all the elaborate provision of military police, ranged to catch the ten per cent, of weaklings that belong to every unit, had no work to do. The Germans themselves were aghast at the cold courage of the advance; and because it was so calm, fantastic stories spread and multiplied through Germany, as indeed through France, of the number of British casualties.

Yet it is not always costly to cross the parapet or charge prepared trenches. Even on 1st July we everywhere reached the German trench in considerable force, even where the distances from trench to trench were widest. We reached, but did not hold. One of the thorniest places thus reached and not held was at the base of the hill south of Thiepval, the crowning citadel above the River Ancre. Nearly two months later I saw intimately, closely, and with the naked eye these same trenches taken at the first intention by comparatively small forces, and with light losses. The excitement of watching such deadly work from a point of almost snug safety was almost intolerable. Tied up securely in that observation point, half a mile behind the charge, I could follow the fortunes of any man I chose; could see the green German figures among the khaki; could watch this man signalling his arrival, this man peering into trenches or holes, or running round a hummock, or chasing an enemy, or sniping.

The sight was so vivid that one wanted to cheer the men on, to shout, "Well played," and to yell applause when praying figures with hands in the air came forward begging mercy. One clean forgot the else intolerable thunder of gun and shell and explosion, and the interval that separated the spectator from the fighter. The human details supplanted even the general progress of the fight and then and there, indeed still, remain the master impression.

As to half the battle, we were attacking the old German front-line system of fortification eastward from the Leipzig Redoubt. Though our two storming parties slightly converged, they went forward to make what was essentially a frontal attack against a line of incalculable strength, backed by half a score of lines no whit less formidable - a mad proceeding, surely. But the method justified the madness; and it is enough to say that within half an hour Headquarters knew that success was ours, that the losses were few and the prisoners numerous.

Those who saw with their eyes the first charge were sure of the victory within five minutes. "I was told in my dugout that the English were attacking. As I came up the steps I met two Englishmen, who said quietly, 'You are our prisoner' - and I was"; so said a German prisoner after an attack on the right: and the same thing happened here in front of my eyes. Virtually the first thing that several score really knew was that they were almost automatically holding up their hands - and this though the attack could not have been a surprise, though the position was as strong as a walled fortress, though a 200 and 300 yards space of pock-marked country, open to direct and enfilade fire, had to be crossed by the attack.

"I have seen or heard nothing which gives me such firm confidence in the British Army," said a foreign observer of wide experience who saw the fight from my vantage-point. But he too, while he watched, was quite absorbed in the human details.

From the parapet of an alley or avenue leading to the maze a single German officer stood erect, motionless, studying without apparent action the defeat in front. He descended into his alley unhurt. Much nearer an English officer appeared, suddenly conspicuous, with his right arm extended, placidly directing his men round a little group of hummocks. A few minutes before three Germans skedaddled away to the left across the open. They were, for me, the first clear, certain, comfortable evidence of easy victory.

Some incidents were almost comic. One English soldier detached himself from a group to chivvy a single German who incontinently fell in a heap before him. We supposed him dead; but not at all. He presently trotted away in the opposite direction as prisoner.

It is the single figure that rivets your eyes, however big the event. In the first charge one of our men stopped, turned round, tottered homewards perhaps for twenty yards, stopped again, turned again, and charged again. He had "pulled himself together," as we say. What wound or shock of shell had checked him no one can tell.

Yet earlier two men from a group on the left fell - one on our side, one on the other - and immediately after the whole group vanished. Men thought with a shiver of all the tales of wholesale destruction by machine-guns; but the glass revealed that they were merely taking cover for a minute. They were soon resurgent and in a trice well on their way up the hill towards Thièpval.

For myself, I could not take my glass off a group of five of our men on the left close to the Leipzig Redoubt. One was a signaller, and I happened to know what his signals meant. Others in front of him looked as if they belonged to a geological picnic. One of them seemed to potter about the humps of earth and chalk as if studying the calcareous strata. One, I fancy, was a sniper. He certainly used his rifle later; but I could find no explanation of the leisured curiosity of the other three. It is a human weakness to think of petty and odd comparisons in the midst of the greatest events and highest excitement. The signaller recalled the flag-carrier on the wing of a line of beaters in a partridge drive, and watching his calm progress in the midst of the hurricane of fire I found myself recalling that Midland beater made famous in *Punch* who said to his neighbour, "How that gentleman do keep pouring the shot into my gaiters, to be sure!"

The crowning moment of the day, for me at any rate, was the sudden appearance of thirty to forty Germans trotting back under guard across the open. They were obviously in so much more of a hurry than anyone who was fighting, always excepting the first Germans to bolt. And they had reason. Another group of them ran straight into a German "crump," exploding with so much smoke and dust that everything round it disappeared. Whether many or any were killed or wounded or buried I have no idea. An inexplicable nervousness possessed another group. They would stop, half turn, hold their hands up again, and then trot on. I suppose they were dazed.

Such incidents as these and many others vibrate in the memory, stand clear in the mind's eye when the bigger things, the exact issue, the battle from the historical aspect, is dull and blurred, a thing best described by some one who was not there.

I had spent perhaps an hour in looking at the battle-field, the multiple German trenches, or rather parapets, mounting in tiers up the hill. Their distinctness and size contrasted abruptly with our tidier line. On the east of the scene, mapped out for the coming battle, a straight valley rises by even gradations till it vanishes into its climax at Mouquet Farm. It was like a shooting gallery. German machine-guns, I knew, pointed down it. For defence the place was ideal, for the attack deadly; and yet the right wing of our advance was preparing to cross it, while the left was delivering the frontal attack on the old German line. Though the right was already across this, they had perhaps the tougher job of the two.

Waiting was interminable. The hands of the watch seemed to refuse to move. All the waiting troops had to see was just the slow, sulky pounding of German lines by our 9.2 howitzers. I could hear their shells but could not see the guns themselves. Occasionally a field battery snapped out in staccato anger one, two, three, four cracks, and the shells sang like angry bees. Very rarely a German 'crump' exploded somewhere in the neighbourhood. That was all.

I had grown tired of looking and listening and expecting when the heavens opened. It was as if some one, as in the legend, had unbarred the cave of the thunder and the winds. You could not, of course, distinguish one gun, one battery from another; but there was just a single standard of comparison or contrast to keep one sane. Two sorts of noise conflicted. Which was louder: the honk and whinny of the shell, splitting the air, or the joint explosions from the gun and from the shell? The nature of the effect was that the thinner, nearer, shrewder noise of the split atmosphere seemed to be laid on the top of the general thud. One coped the other.

The shrapnel and the high explosive, bursting over the German trenches, gave a similar impression in the domain of sight. The wicked lightning of the shrapnel, bursting extremely low, topped the heavy smoke and earthy columns from the heavy shells. For a few seconds I could distinguish separate hits: a shrapnel that raked an alley, a heavy shell that struck a parapet; but such distinctions were soon wiped out. The valley, "the shooting gallery," running towards Mouquet, even the line of scarred trees that stand for Thièpval, were lost in smoke; and in front a mass of fumes and dust moved like a great cumulus cloud before the western wind, and as it moved it was ever renewed at the base.

The hither side, or No Man's Land, was quite clear; and with what seemed an ecstasy of splendid suicide our men left the shelter of their trench and charged straight for the furnace. By what sleight of hand the furnace withdrew before them, like a rainbow you chase, is impossible to say. Some one certainly played the magician that day. The military fact that stands out was the level accuracy and slick timing of an artillery fire of incomparable volume and intensity. It left the Germans dead and blind and dazed. For a while the gabble of machine-guns broke through the thunder of guns and shells; but they were soon stilled.

I do not think that I saw any of our men killed by gunfire, though some were visible coming back wounded from the trenches; and twice a German shell quite hid a group of men as it burst on the nearer side. A mere spectator does not, of course, see the more terrible side. A man falls, and that is all; and the fall itself is not very obvious, but our losses were slight - to use the statistical word - especially slight in reaching and crossing this powerful line in front of me.

I fixed my glass on one small group on the left and saw them reach the front trench and cross it without losing a man. They went straight on without pause, and were still undiminished when I lost them behind some heaps and turned to a wider view. How I should like to know their individuality, especially of that left-hand signaller!

It is possible to watch a battle, even to fight in it, and afterwards know very little indeed of what happened. It was so on 1st July. Half the first impressions by corps and army observers were wrong. There was a mist and our men went too fast. But this small battle was as I saw it. The casualties over all the left part of the attack in front of me were exactly twenty-three. They were only seventy on the right, where "the shooting gallery" was crossed. If I had not seen it I should not have believed the possibility.

We took a fortress. We secured over two hundred prisoners. We killed an unknown number of men: fifty German bodies were counted, apart from those buried by shells and in dugouts. The fire on the attacked trenches was very deadly, and one massed counter-attack was scattered.

We took trenches over a front of nearly 1000 yards to a depth of 300 to 400 yards. All this was done at the rush against every handicap in the nature of the ground, with a loss of under one hundred during the attack. All we had to help us in natural conditions was sun and wind, which made observation almost perfect.

Within an hour or two I had some glimpse of the battle through the enemy's eyes. Among the prisoners was one soldier who had just come from Verdun. "That," he said, "was bad, but nothing to the Somme!" Very much the same opinion, given in reference to artillery fire, came from other Germans taken a day or two earlier, and the truth is that every battle is worse than its forerunner. The world accelerates its gallop to destruction. A few days later I saw this attack repeated with equal success. It was a day of heavy fighting elsewhere; but nowhere did the ground offer such advantages for observation. The bare and regular acclivities leading to the skeleton trees and dead houses of Thièpval allowed one to watch every movement of troops, every yard of trench, and the pitch of individual shells.

Once again our good, steady English troops went over the parapet and marched their way methodically into one German trench after another, bombing and taking prisoners as they went. Once again within a few minutes of the attack little frightened groups of the enemy ran the gauntlet of their own barrage and dashed for safety to their enemy's lines. But strangely similar though the issues were in these two successive attacks, both northwards by "the Leipzig salient" toward Thièpval, they differed by the poles for the soldier who "jumped the lid," and even to the observer. For a battle-field is not like a map, though something may be inferred from the map.

The contour of the hill is a regular rise. On the Monday we climbed; on Thursday we nearly reached the 460-feet level which marks the top of the ridge. For a certain number of the troops the uphill battle (in the literal sense) was over when their charge finished. They were on ground virtually as high as Thièpval itself.

By a lucky accident I reached my vantage-point just at the moment when our artillery opened. The suddenness was that of a near clap of thunder succeeding occasional low and distant growls, but the bombardment had not - so it seemed to me - quite the sharp definition, the portcullis effect. Its sphere seemed wider and the individual shell more notable. Some separate explosions would have stood out, distinct and terrible, in any bombardment, even in a Vesuvian eruption.

I had just fixed my glass on a certain German strong point when a great shell hit it full. A black and sepia rush of foul smoke shot up into the shape of a sweep's brush, out topping all other explosions by many yards. Then from the edges of this toadstool of smoke solid things began to drop; black oblongs and rhomboids and shapeless lumps. What they were, mortal or material, I do not know, nor what created the immensity of this explosion. Later in the day I saw nearer at hand a white and yellow cloud rise to double this height without ever losing its uncanny shape, which suggested an anatomical picture of the human brain. But that was almost beautiful beside this black, repulsive phenomenon. Huge though it was, for the moment dominating the hill-side, it was after all not twice as big as scores of other explosions whose effect was solely produced by their own explosive.

Thièpval itself was like a forest fire, in which the fumes and smoke had taken the colours of the autumnal leaves - "yellow and black and pale and hectic red." The colours fit the scheme exactly; the line needs no alteration. And through and past the smother came the German shells, creating a second though lesser fire. One little patch of earth just opposite me was suddenly churned up by two salvos of 5.9 or some such weight of gun. The eight shells exploded within a minute or two of one another, a very few minutes after our guns had opened against the Thièpval orchard trees. The salvos were useless: but had the shells fallen in the midst of our advancing infantry, they would have made no manner of difference to the steadiness of the advance.

Of all that I have ever seen, the most unforgettable, the most impressive, a thing that must make an Englishman always proud to be English and most grateful to the Englishmen of to-day, is the sight of our soldiers marching forward through such shell fire without deviating a foot, without showing sign or symptom that the shell - exploding, as it seems, at their elbows - had any danger or terror in it. Yet such a shell can pitch a bar of railway metal 100 yards and shoot the solid base of its own case nearly half a mile, and the havoc of the destroyed ground is clearly visible at 1500 yards. Nevertheless, English troops walk through such little obstacles with less disturbance of mind or manner than a wasp creates at a breakfast table.

I had watched Gloucestershire troops so march in solid majesty up the lower slopes of this shattered hill during the first attack. This day the men who did it came from neighbour counties: from Worcestershire, which earned fame in the attack on Contalmaison, and from Wiltshire, whose men had fought most stolidly round Pozières, as at every spot where they have been pitched. They said of themselves that the English have greater reputation in defence than in attack. "The old county troops always stick it out and always will" - that is what every one says of them, and what they feel of themselves.

The truth of the maxim was to be proved to the hilt the very night after the attack. The noise and tumult of the German fire before me on the hill-side was more than doubled the following evening; and "contracted into a span" on our newly won trenches. On its heels followed picked troops of the Prussian Guard, those would-be masters of the world. But their dominant name made as little difference as had the brutal explosive to the steadfastness of our English troops. They had been hammered. They were battle tired. They had charged and fought and dug. They were hammered again. But when the Prussian Guard, brought up fresh for the purpose, came to the charge, these immovable troops were as ready for the men as the shells. Seldom was the motto better kept: "What we have, we hold." The truth was recorded in set terms by the Germans themselves, perhaps in reference to these attacks, through the report of Von Armin. "The English," he wrote, "show surprising skill in holding and organizing a conquered position."

The spectacle of the infantry was so absorbing that all other parts of the battle were like to be forgotten. But to see a modern battle one must look up as well as down. It is easy to forget the air. I remember in watching the second British attack up the hill towards Thièpval, and among a pattern of trenches known as the Wonder Work, I saw, but nearly missed, a spectacular detail full both of beauty and meaning. Lifting my eyes a moment from the battle among the ditches, I caught sight of one of our aeroplanes. It served as pointer to another and then another until the sky seemed full of them, all quite inaudible through the noise of the guns. Some were high, some comparatively low. No German gun could shoot without drawing their eagle eye to it, and no German plane come near to return the compliment, to spy upon our fire. Thanks to them, our artillery hit over a score of enemy emplacements that very day.

What happened in the air above me was this. These circling eagles of ours saw one German plane, greatly daring, though skied inconceivably high, making towards our line. In a moment their dilettante circling ceased, and the flock steered a straight course for the enemy. "Up and at 'em" is at least as true of the British airman as of the British soldier. "Down and away" was the only possible answer of the German; and he took his only alternative with admirable celerity.

Our airmen always thus gather to a battle. They have strange experiences. Again and again when the storm breaks they see the thunderbolt. Our great howitzer shells at the top of their flight are perfectly visible, and even give the impression of not travelling at any inordinate speed. As the war goes on many airmen find that they see a score of things previously invisible. They know what to look for; and perhaps they become attuned to what they work in, gaining a technical as well as a spacious vision. How much their universal presence, their eyes as well as their missiles, have affected the enemy's emotions we know from many letters and other evidence.

So even in a close and local attack on trenches the airmen play their part and make beneficent journeys over the infantry. But one hardly heeds them. It is difficult to attend to any part of the field except where the infantry are engaged, especially in a fight of this nature. One forgets the artillery itself if a single righting soldier is visible.

Even the spectacle of war which I saw by Thièpval, where our men climbed tier by tier over the German trenches before my eyes, was surpassed by a fighting picture visible a few days later over the spur of Falfemont Farm and the valley of Wedge Wood on our right wing.

The waterspouts of rain which elsewhere quenched all the fires of war here stirred it into activity. In a small field and in a succession of skirmishes were concentrated all the pomp and circumstance of antique warfare, soiled and muddled as always by dirt, dust, and confusion.

From a point behind Guillemont you could see French troops sweeping forward in triumphant lines on the right, while our men were clearing the great dugouts of Guillemont, sending back their hundreds of prisoners and bombing here and there among trenches. While news was just beginning to spread of a French forward sweep away over the Somme, and our men were firm in their defences beyond Guillemont - the centre of the view, the event on which eyes centred, was an enemy's charge to recover and keep the precious ridged slope close by the ravine where we and the French join hands.

No episode in the war has so dwelt on the brain of those who witnessed it as a suicidal charge of the Prussian Guard near Ypres two years before. Two hundred men swung round a plantation into our view, in one close rank, arm locked in arm, and rifle slung over the shoulder, and holding their left arms across their eyes. All were shot down. They almost repeated the scene, though this was fighting, not suicide, against troops commanded by the same British general who saw the annihilation of that storming party at Ypres. Yet no two settings for a drama of war could have been less like.

The stage in the Somme battle was an undulating and beautiful stretch of French country - its framework an artificial triangle. At the top was Leuze Wood, a close-knit grove, not then unleafed and dismantled by inveterate shelling. Southward from it runs a clear-cut ridge for a thousand yards, ending, for my purpose, in Falfemont Farm. Let the base of the triangle run westwards from this down a quick slope to Wedge Wood, which blocks the base of the valley. Guillemont lies distinct as a wall pattern on the left and Falfemont on the right.

At the farm and the wood the attack had been held up on the previous day; and when on the morrow we renewed the attack a battle of the older sort sprang into view. It was fought for the most part not in trenches but in the open. In the open, men conquered or died. The place was an oasis, a home of respite from the terrors of shell fire elsewhere universal. Neither side had freedom enough of knowledge or vision to be sure of its target. Germans came out with the bayonet to face our charging troops, and the righting was everywhere hand to hand. It is hardly necessary to say that the machine-guns rattled and gabbled almost continuously.

One of our waves that marched in very open order up the slope to Falfemont met the fire from the strong points about the farm, and was covered - as in much of this fighting - by screens of our machine-gun fire. Apart from these clear and traceable lines of attack - now against the farm, now past the wood and up to the V of trenches beyond - odd and occasional groups of men moved in eccentric orbits. Three or four would scuttle away from the farm along the spur. A few others - were they prisoners? - moved southwards, and were thought to be carrying a white flag. To and fro moved this restless patrol of battle on the ridge and the slope of the valley. It seemed inextricable, when, as if finally to straighten out the tangle and assert dominance, a new power entered.

From the neighbourhood of Leuze Wood appeared in closed, perfect formation, arm touching arm, if not arm linked in arm, the leaders of a battalion of German troops, a reserve of the Prussian Guard. Appearing and disappearing in the varying sinuosities of the ground and growths that cover it, they advanced steadily, scarcely, if at all, touched by shell fire, till they reached the range of our rifles and machine-guns. They faced the music. They met the blare, so it seemed, and quite perished under it. At least, they vanished.

Other waves followed, and our men appeared to retreat a little way. Soon the fight fell back into confusion again. The serried phalanx had failed to bring Prussian order or dominance into the turbulence of the melee. What was the end? We seemed to have won the wood and beyond it, and to have some footing at least in the farm. The righting had no visible end when the afternoon gloom of a stormy day took away the vision.

The facts of the victory were known that night; but they were not felt till two days later, when it was possible to visit the battle-field. Across the slope the Prussian dead lay in some score among the rank grass of the hill-side; and nearer Guillemont, just to the east of it, our photographers were taking pictures of a trench where forty dead lay heaped one on the other within as many yards. Yet this was a small skirmish of little account in a day of great fighting.

A return along the corridors leading to the battle itself gives a more telling picture of what war is than the distant sight of actual infantry engagement. Wounded as they hobble back or are borne on stretchers, the groups of prisoners, the distant sight of fighting men, the blast of guns and burst of shells, the sight of a landscape turned to a volcano of a hundred craters, the knowledge of the numbers engaged - all this and other noisy evidence may give an observer a more poignant sense of the meaning of the war than even the sight of a charge, though, I suppose, it is only the soldier who crosses the parapet and endures the thunderbolts directed against him who can know how great a thing he has done, and if he is a British soldier he will hardly confess his knowledge.

CHAPTER VIII
THE NEW FIGHTING

I HAVE NO ambition to follow geographically or in any successive detail the twenty weeks' campaign opened on the morning of the 1st July. Every battalion, every brigade, every division has a war diary, much of it supplied by company commanders. One of the hundred labours that falls to the lot of the regimental officer is the compilation of this record immediately he comes out of the righting. Indeed, he must make notes even while fighting. The full skeleton of the story is in these; the bones, if not the flesh and blood; and the skeleton will one day be dressed in full historical canonicals.

Though I heard the news daily, and daily saw, sometimes from near, sometimes from far, the course of the battle, and read many diaries and talked daily with the men who had come fresh from the battle, my ambition is rather to give some faint idea of the meaning and complexion of the war, so far as it came within my own experience, rather than any continuous narrative of its formal progress. When we are near events, all that is worth much is the harvest of our eyes and ears. Judgments follow later.

When we broke the German line at Mametz and Montauban, and pinched out Fricourt, we took a fortress and stormed ramparts that only months of labour could raise or rather sink. This was obvious long before one scrambled down stairs and passages into the chambers of the fort, and peered through the armoured lantern slits in the earth barriers. But my imagination at any rate had never leaped to the depth and extension of the change that the victory was to bring in its train. The heaping up of force and material behind our lines had been palpable enough for many weeks, but it had all been cloaked and subdued.

Suddenly, as it seemed, the ground became yeasty with activity of all sorts. The valley and slopes spawned horses and mules. The country was like a circus. Whole valleys filled up with the deposit of war: horses, mules, limbers, lorries, tents, huts, wire cages. Ambulances, guns, and marching troops overflowed the edges of the roads. Guns lurched forward on the trail of the enemy, arriving mysteriously at impossible sites. Khaki figures in quantity wandered about, as if for pleasure or curiosity, all over the battle-field, as if shells were as unknown as they were undreaded. On 3rd July, as I entered Fricourt and turned sick at the sight of the dead bodies, a great part of the hill-side to my left was alive with men: engineers, pioneers, road-makers, reserve patrols, artillery prospectors, even here and there an unauthorized souvenir hunter dotted the whole slope. It was quite a new thing to find soldiers in the open close to the enemy. For nearly two years no one had left the|trenches except to cross dead ground. Some avenues were miles long, and it was thought fatal to leave their concealment. You were inevitably sniped, if not with rifles, with field artillery. For so many months every one, both soldier and observer, had sidled forward up these ditches that the return to the open life was as surprising as it was pleasant. It was difficult to grow used to the idea; but the press and stir were as the breath of hope, and bred a high confidence in all the world.

Nor was the sense of excitement visibly depressed at all by the broken wagons and dead horses and mules, and occasional eruptions of dust and dirt and smoke from the scattered shells of the enemy. The world seemed so wide that each atom was safe. Men felt for the nonce, as they looked to the airmen, so wide apart, that no one man was likely to be hit. For the master impression from the air is of an empty world. On the ground where you see a road or a camp in rank or in perspective, the more distant dots close up against the nearer; a platoon or two, a horse or cart or two, obscure the gaps between them. From the air the intervals have thus full value. Even these massed camps, which gave the impression of a whole people on migration, - a race of nomads stopping their march for a day or two, - had a scattered look. Your impression was that a bomb dropped would miss the horses and the huts nine times out of ten.

But even from high in the air there are relative emptinesses. All through this battle of the Somme the contrast between the German side of the line and ours was quite incredibly abrupt. Our army with all its appurtenances might be encamped on the edge of a desert with the trenches dividing "the desert from the sown." Behind the enemy's line is just emptiness: you see no horses, no lorries, no limbers, no moving troops. Even the air is emptier. In an unbroken line over our camps the great sausage balloons swing and sway, looking vastly, if deceptively, numerous.

All this emptiness on the ground or above it was to the credit of the airmen. The German troops, the German ground, the German stores moved at night and only at night. Scarcely a lorry dared open itself to the eyes of the airmen, who would as lief as not glide down and use their machine-guns as if they were infantry. Doubtless the clever use made of railways - heavy and light railways, trench railways, munition railways - helped the enemy to empty his roads and withdraw his camps; and his tricks of concealment, of *camouflage* are various and clever, though never so good as the French. But sheer fear of our aircraft was the chief cause of the utter inanity of the country within a mile or two of the front. You saw there literally nothing; and by reason of the contrast returned to wonder yet more at the stir and freedom of open-air life behind the British army.

The side that is least afraid will win - that was the first thought a trip in the air left with me. But this German fear of being seen was not integral to the warfare; it was no more than the dominance of our airmen, acting as eyes to an artillery much superior in weight and volume. But on both sides all the time, thousands upon thousands of men, with no immediate concern in the righting, are living under shell fire; on our side in the open, on the German under flimsy coverings. The strangeness is that the battle-field has no boundaries, no definition; and who shall say which part is more or less dangerous, where danger begins and ends? I know a general of cavalry, who has flitted much from one part of the line to another, who maintains that the only safe place is No Man's Land. The jest has some meaning in it. When once you worm your way to the forward sap, you are like to be free from shell fire, and in the course of an advance are probably safe from the trench mortar.

But No Man's Land is not easy to reach. You must pass through a strip two to three miles long, all of which is under shell fire, though most of it seems and, in the normal course, is as "healthy" as you would wish. Yet who knows? One day, as I drove to this beckoning battle-field, I met the signs of German shells twelve miles behind our front line. "Whistling Percy," as the men call the smaller naval shells, had picked the spot out as target the day before. A mile or more nearer the front not a house was touched, never had been touched. The traffic was so thick that the traffic N.C.O.'s and an A.P.M. (from the Peerage) were playing as busy a part as the policemen at Charing Cross. After crawling, at the pace of the brigade marching in front, for another five miles or more, past fields trampled to sheer earth by horses, past tents and dugouts and dumps and old gun emplacements and heaps of used shell cases covering half an acre, and strings of artillery horses I reached a hill-top from which the smoke of bursting shells was visible, but at a distance too great for any distinctive noise. I had passed some of our own longer-ranged guns, which fired at rare intervals; but the place hardly suggested immediate battle. Cars could still proceed a mile or two farther, if need be, and do no harm. As we sat in the car discussing whether to leave the car here and desert the roads and walk across country, a quick, angry squeak was heard almost simultaneously with a sharp explosion. It seemed a meaningless thing that had arrived by accident. Near though it was, it hardly suggested real war. A firework would have made more fuss. But men were running forward to the spot; and a few minutes later four of them passed, carrying a soldier with one leg completely shattered.

It was still difficult to believe the reality of this accident, for it made no difference to anything. No one changed his occupation, or amusement, except perhaps ourselves; and we drove the car to another spot farther on and went on with the programme. We walked some two miles nearer the battle, sheering off from one road which the Germans patrolled with a succession of 5.9 shells; but no shell came again within half a mile or more of us. Occasionally and in places men have walked straight across the open into the front trench without any sense of running great risk. The next day a mouse could scarcely escape through one or other of the stretches along which they passed.

At no point anywhere - or so it may be - is there any division to tell you where in the battlefield you are. The guns are sprinkled here, there, and everywhere in no scheme, no order, some pointing one way, some another. Trenches are many, some half filled up, some like newly cut drains, but nothing exactly indicates which is old and disused and German, which meant as an alley. Both are deserted; and on you tramp round and about the rugged shell holes or past the rubble of houses or through the fractured woods without any definite notion of the neighbourhood of the enemy or the degree of danger. This vagueness is often worse quite near the front, where trenches are a necessary refuge, at any rate by day. Not once or twice the infantry have prevented artillery observers walking straight into the net of the enemy's sniper if not the enemy's trench. Two observers about the time of this journey I write of found themselves long before they expected in the front trench, and were warned to go no farther, as the enemy's sharp-shooters were very active. One took no heed, and was killed almost instantly, not, as it happened, by a bullet, but by a field-gun shell. The other, after recovering the body, did his business and returned. He had run great risk and was now, he thought, safe, but decided to cling to the trench a little longer. Half a minute after his decision a 5.9 shell hit the trench full and buried him completely. The arrival of a platoon of infantry alone saved his life; and they spent a full hour in the work of digging him out. Who shall say where safety or danger is found?

All is different in the common trench warfare. It may be more dangerous behind the head of the communication trench than in it; but at least distances and divisions are well denned. At a certain spot you enter an alley, generally well revetted with V-shaped boards and wire and whatnot, and walk for the rest of the way, it may be two miles, down and along the ditch, except where now and again it sinks into dead ground. In the new warfare-half stagnant, half mobile - there was never time to build the regular alley or communication trench. Sometimes the front line was itself far from being a continuous trench in the old sense. Either the captured line had been so knocked out of shape by our artillery as to lose all coherence, or we had fortified a new line by joining up shell holes as best we could. Some important places much exposed to shell fire, especially that scorched sky-line from Mouquet farm to Thièpval and the windmill along the Bapaume road, were entirely held by posts; and no one less than a genius could tell quite exactly how the fringe of these posts ran. When the Canadians relieved the Australians in this district they altogether failed to find some of the men, who drifted back from scattered shell holes during the next two or three days. In this fighting, the separate soldier was thrown on his own resources. His use and his safety depended on his wits and courage all day and every day.

The difficulty of relieving the posts and above all of removing men wounded in the posts or alleged trenches might be insuperable. The very courage of the stretcher-bearers - often aided by the pioneers - itself increased the trouble, so many of the men fell in their self-sacrificing work. Stories there are of human affection in this fighting which take their place alongside any of the immortal friendships in fight - of Roland and Oliver, or of Jonathan and David; but the names will never go down to history, for often one man did not know the other's name. An Australian who had done most things in many lands and brought his experience to this war, found himself in charge of one of the advanced posts, and lived a lifetime within three days. He wished to hold the place and yet never to fire, for fear of giving away too useful knowledge to the enemy. The strain was extreme, and the men must be relieved from it every eight hours or so. It was as dangerous to relieve by night as by day. One of the first men to come out kicked one of the German bombs that smothered the obliterated saps and shell holes, and was mortally wounded. The Australian captain of the post went out, bound him up as best he could, and gave him water in answer to his pitiful cries. "You haven't a chance with your waterbottle," said the Australian in recalling the incident. "Properly we are not allowed to give 'em drink of any sort, but what can you do when they're wailing for water, water, all about you?"

He himself was taking his turn at this pernicious hole (sharing in the glory of holding our farthest advance at the highest point), when a shower of bombs descended. The Germans had crept up on several sides, "or it might have been our own men from the next lot, you never can tell. Some of the bits looked very like a Mills." He was hit in some dozen places: in the legs, arms and bowel-walls. But being a man of great heart and rough life he could force his limbs to move, and he walked away to seek a dressing station. He moved with infinite pain perhaps half or a quarter of a mile an hour, but even at this pace lost his way; and after six hours lay down in a little sap, spitting out from some trench or other, to sleep or die. Somehow, somewhere, some one joined him: if not a god, a man of great heart and stature, and indeed beauty. "Come along, mate. I know the way," he said. But the Australian could not move and could not endure the pain of being moved. "You go," he said. "I'm done in, and maybe a stretcher-bearer will come along sometime." But Oliver refused, and what the Australian could not do for himself, he did for the friend. After half an hour or so, the miracle was wrought: the man got up and walked - more slowly, more painfully than before. It was now light, and every few yards the sap was blown in, so that the two must face the open. "You hurry over and I'll follow as best I can," said Roland; but Oliver would have none of it. "We go together. If you've got to have it, I'll have it too." So arm in arm they crept over the mud barriers and heard the steel bullets of the snipers ring by them. After many hours, they hit a trench full of wounded. The stretcher-bearers had suffered, had started work rather late, so intense was the German barrage, and the work was slow to the point of madness. The wounded could not be carried for the other wounded who lay on the floor of the ditch. The only way was to lift these men out into the open, doubly exposed to further wounds, that their companions could be carried back. So this pair of wanderers, too brave to add to the burden of the day, left the trench for the open, and waded on arid on for another two or three hours, one of them longing to lie down and die, but aware that if he stopped he would never get up again. He had long ago quite given up the attempt to make his companion leave him. At last the journey that had lasted a great part of the night and day was over. An orderly at an advanced dressing station saw them and gathered them into the hospitality of a wide dugout. The two men never met again, are still ignorant each of the other's name or battalion, but - greater love has no man than this - The Australian's life was saved by an immediate operation, the first of a long series. I saw him months afterwards, at home, when most of the bits of bombs were removed and his colour was restored, and told one of the nurses a part of his story. "I don't know what we should do without him," she answered. "He cuts up the dinner of every one who can't manage, and is kind as a woman." The reason in part is that this rough warrior, whose face is knocked out of shape by fights in far corners of the world and whose skin is roughened by exposure in tramp steamers in all weathers - has a love, "passing the love of woman," for the man or god who journeyed with him across the putrid craters of that nightmare highland in France.

The new fighting called out every quality in the soldier and the officer. It was a joint war of movement and of siege, and each fortress was of a different sort: a wood, a village, an earth-defence, a sunken road. All the while artillery was moving, and behind the first troops lines of movement built and strengthened and cleared. Each great leap forward was prepared by continuous fights for position, by digging saps, by isolated attacks, by patrol work and continuous study of the enemy's lines, especially from the air. Photography from the air, the piecing of the maps, the reading of the maps became a new subject calling for specialists at headquarters. Every one was learning new things about war every day, soldiers and corps-commanders alike, for nine out of ten of , the attributes of warfare were new. The schools had not taught them and no man had experienced them. Aircraft and the concentration of heavy artillery had exploded established theories, and introduced not only new problems but new diseases, new demands on the human machine.

CHAPTER IX
THE SIX WOODS

O N 3rd JULY I crept with many fears into the edge of Fricourt
Wood, past the dressing station and into the trees. It had not
greatly suffered. The place was "pinched out" and for some reason no
superlative shelling of the place had been decreed by either side. Twenty
thousand shells and more may have burst there, perhaps a hundred
thousand; but into Delville on the last day of a six weeks' bombardment
we emptied at least a hundred and twenty thousand; and they were
concentrated only on one section. The bombardment was the heaviest
till then attempted. Fricourt was, in the soldier's phrase, a health resort,
a phrase meaning that life there was endurable. Ypres during the Somme
battle was a "health resort." You were not quite sure to be shelled in the
open, the approaches were open the greater part of the day, and only
now and then was any section of trench knocked into hummocks. In
that sense Fricourt was a health resort for a few days after the battle.
Bernafay Wood, to the east of Montauban, was another health resort,
just for a while. Only alleys, no fire trenches ran through it. We captured
it in twenty minutes with not as many as fifty casualties. But Bernafay,
taken much at the same time as Fricourt, became a day later a roosting-
place for innumerable shells; and many men died there. At least as often
as not it is more costly to hold than to take.

But we had not yet tasted the full terror of the woods; nor had the
Germans yet learned the full art of their defence. They had abandoned
Fricourt and Bernafay at too great a speed; and had left no feeding pipe
for the reinforcement of the garrison. Their revenge at Bernafay was
to sentinel our approaches with a quite ceaseless *chassé* of heavy shells.
Almost every day for a while I went within sight and hearing of this
wood; and not once was there intermission of the bark of 5.9 shells
and the black columns rising with damnable iteration from the hither

edge of the wood. And then as ever afterwards throughout the battle they fired rather more at night than by day. Woods are the delight of attacking and despair of the defending artillery. Every contact shell that hits a tree is likely to explode. It follows that a shell becomes dangerous several hundred yards before it reaches its target.

Before the 15th September, when the last of the woods on our front was captured, and London troops put the final flourish on our knowledge in High Wood, we were to know all there was to be known about wood fighting.

When we forced a way into High Wood and pressed over the ridge down the slope facing the enemy our own gunners were helpless. The enemy facing us rested in a pool of serenity where no shells broke - for this reason. Any contact shell directed on their lines was more likely than not to strike a tree in its course over British trenches and explode its fragments suicidally. The Germans were as safe as a man sheltering under the arch of a waterfall; and in this case, owing to the fall of the ground, the cascade fell many hundred yards beyond them. But for hostile artillery a wood is a perfect target, that no one can miss, though it is a little difficult to detect the exact location of emplacements and trenches. For the men the cover adds to the terror. Shells strike and explode above ground on the trunks. Every burst is endowed with a longer life of noise and higher intensity. Fragments fly at all tangents and, above all, the discovery and recovery of wounded men is a nightmare. To hear them calling at night through the wizardry of the tangled trees and roots fills the strongest with a shivering pity, like no other sensation in war.

Retreat in a wood surpasses all endurance, for it adds horror to the bitterest sensation a man knows: the compulsion to leave his wounded behind. Men are doubly brave in victory, largely because they know if they fall that they will be found and fetched, salved or saved, by their own people. It may not be so with all peoples - with the Latins, who have a gift of stronger intellectual imagination and higher mental ecstasy, but with English county troops the sense of staying alive or dead with their own people buttresses their courage more than any other single cause; and nothing so depresses, so saddens them as the thought that they have left their friends wounded within the pale of the enemy or, yet worse, in No Man's Land. The flourish set on the brutality of war is the abandonment of wounded men to die slowly of cold, of hunger, of decay. Men have been brought into hospital after eight days of exposure when they have eaten and drunken only such scraps and drops as they could filch after dolorous crawling in the mire from the dead who were their companions.

And every wood across our path, except the first two, we nearly won and largely lost, not once, but many times, before trenches were fortified on the farther side, and the whole made good. Each of these woods is holy ground: Trônes, Mametz, Delville, and the Bois des Foureaux or High Wood; the cradle of high fame, as well as the grave of many noble lives. Troops from every part of Britain fought these forest fights.

It has come about that each wood is associated with a particular regiment; and though perhaps a score of others fought as hard, the fame has always been won by signal service and a bloody fight.

The West Kents claim Trônes by virtue of their forty-eight hours' siege, but in Trônes the worst of the fighting was the endurance of the shells by those who occupied it. One morning a young Fusilier officer was sitting there with the regimental doctor, also a young man; and while the heavy shells burrowed and barked and, gobbled among the tree roots all round them, they discussed the war, which both hated. The doctor was, and happily is, one of the best of the younger bacteriologists, and the officer a great lover of field natural history. There the two crouched in the dark - for the shell explosions perpetually blew out the candle - feeling themselves negative, if not useless, doing the work of a clod of earth, and likely at any moment to be pulverized by the ploughshare.

"It seems a pity" said the doctor at last, "that you should like all you like, and I should know all I know, and we two be HERE."

So at all sorts of times and places does the futility of war breed revolt in the finer spirits; but always everywhere it is the finer spirit that holds out best, and best bears the brutality of shelling. That has been proved in this war times without number.

Trônes Wood introduced to us the grimness of wood fighting. The

Germans bordered it on our side with heavy shells, and kept all the while within their grip a few trenches by which they could filter into the fastnesses at will. As soon as our infantry came within attacking distance of these reinforced garrisons, our artillery was forced to withdraw its defence, and the enemy was left with the upper hand. The pear shape of the wood forced attacking troops to move from different directions, and, as experience in Delville afterwards proved (indeed, as we had already proved on the way from the Marne to the Aisne two years before), even regular soldiers could scarcely avoid the risk of firing at each other. Before my own eyes, as a foreboding picture of wood fighting, I keep the memory of a single English soldier who fell to English bullets in a little wood above the Marne, where his body was found as I reached the field nearly three weeks later.

Trônes Wood remained an unspeakable cemetery for many weeks, for there, backwards and forwards, our troops and the Germans ebbed and flowed, each wave leaving behind it dead and wounded tangled in the undergrowth, like the bodies of seagulls mixed with other flotsam in the sea-wrack on a leeward shore.

Our own wounded and German wounded each in turn underwent a heavy shelling from their own guns. In some cases - I know one incredible experience - the wounded of the two sides fought duels with one another while they lay or crouched in the undergrowth or in craters, all the while increased promiscuously by either artillery. The intensity of our fire on one section of this cemetery was visible from miles away before the final attack, and the pillars of smoke served for a suitable background to the flashes and clouds of the enemy's shrapnel barraging on the near side.

Mametz Wood, taken almost at the same time was in some ways worse, because bigger; and

"Enter these enchanted woods,
Ye who dare."

The Germans had stretched wires like poacher's snares. They had cut paths and avenues for hidden machine-guns to rake. They had built caves of Cacus and bristling forts - all this in a forest of exceptional thickness through which you would hardly care to push merely for the spidery and weevil fustiness of it.

It was repulsive then and afterwards. As I pushed through it some days after its capture the flies had settled like a thick, sticky sediment at the bottom of the shell holes. Once when I jumped into one on the sound of a singing shell, they lifted some few inches, like a coverlet raised by a puff of wind, and then settled back in their original position. Among the horrors of the wood was the wreck of one of our own aeroplanes.

The wood held us up for many days after the first rush through the nearer half; and a second brilliant attack from the eastern side, which I watched on a day of such singular clearness that I could see the shadows of the juniper's bushes at a distance sufficient to reduce the men to the size of beetles. The delay caused much heart-searching, for we wished to hurry on to the second great attack finally delivered on 14th July and nothing could be done till Mametz was ours. It fell at last to Welsh troops, including the London Welsh. The men were perhaps peculiarly sensitive to the diabolism of the place. One platoon of these gallant Welshmen were waiting for the moment of attack with tingling nerves, when one of their officers fired a Verey-light cartridge from his pistol. At the top of its flight it lit the jagged trunks looking like giant skeletons, and as it fell, as it almost touched the undergrowth, it lit not a skeleton but a live giant. The face was shown up, clear and ghostly, and the body seemed to partake of the enormity of the trees. The young officer, himself constantly afraid of being afraid as are many brave men, had some ado to stop a real panic. For the first and only time his men began to run away, but the crisis was momentary. The light died down, and from the ambush of a tree a petrified voice cried out, "Mercy, Kamerad" The figure of fear was a German deserter.

Within a wood all the common sounds and symptoms of war gain terror. The sense of direction of sound is blurred or distorted. When these gallant Welshmen were delivering their final triumphant attack, a single German machine-gun opened fire in the extreme corner of the wood. Its deadly tap seemed placeless, everywhere and yet nowhere, echoing off trunks and thrown back by blocks of trees. This single gun, which was firing not into the wood but across the open, almost arrested the charge. There was one moment of wavering and then the terror was converted into an ecstasy of rage. The Welshmen bitted their imagination and drove straight through the northern space of the wood, across the trench at the edge and so out into the open.

Thus the wood was won; but it was not cleared. Two days later a German officer was discovered in a dugout with stores of food, with maps and telephone apparatus; and there is some evidence that he amused himself with occasional sniping. The clearance work of any battle-field is both laborious and repulsive. An attack to-day means so much more than an attack. First, behind an attacking force in this war, come "the cleaners," as the French call them, who follow into trenches and dugouts and rake out or burn out or bomb out or smoke out the hiders and the ambuscaders lying in wait in holes and earths. After those who attend to the remnant of the living come the men whose work it is to look after the dead. But a wood surpasses a trench, and in this great rectangle was no end to the strange discoveries, from the short necked howitzer, which could not be pulled from its lair, to all the pitiful litter of retreat and defeat.

Like other captured woods, it contained near the northern end a huge dump for food, letters, and ammunition. Prisoners surrendering here and in similar places speak with peculiar horror of the thirst they suffered. In Fricourt Wood men were saved from something near madness by the thunder rain that made pools in their trenches. Water is almost always the hardest of supplies to send through a barrage. Imagine the position of a German soldier shackled by foot and waist to his machine-gun when the water-carriers failed; and other soldiers, as tied by discipline as he by chains, fare little better. A letter found on one of the prisoners said: "We are shut off from the rest of the world. Nothing comes to us. No letters. The enemy keeps such a barrage on all the communications. It's terrible."

For ourselves, when we had taken the place and held it firm, with trenches out beyond, the wood remained a place of ill-omen. Cavalrymen and yeomen who went up to help clear and dig trenches never turned their hand to less lovely employment. Every day and most of the day the enemy, who knew every inch of the wood, directed their guns on to crucial spots. Every day and nearly all day you could see the great black columns rising from the scarred trees, and hurling dark lumps, which one prayed were no more than wood and stone, high into air. Here General Williams was killed.

After five months the whole of the wood is probably not explored. Even one of the guns was not discovered for several weeks.

THE STORY OF DELVILLE WOOD

The occupation of Mametz and Trônes left us free to attack a wood that was to have and keep an ugly pre-eminence. In the course of that most brilliant attack of 14th July the two Bazentin woods and villages were captured and held "at the first instance" by our left and centre; and the right wing began with equal dash and fortune. The village of Longueval, nursed under the western lea of the wood, was penetrated, and our South African troops - the most highly trained, the most athletic men that ever I saw - swept across the wood. Their charge, in spite of its triumph, was no more than the prelude to a six weeks' battle, much of it fought on the edges of the wood, which was completely ditched in. But no association of troops, no acts of regimental daring surpassed the combination of South African and Scottish troops in the early fighting.

The South Africans rushed the wood, but the Germans held all the approaches, many of them quite protected from hostile shell fire. The remnants of the South Africans who coursed through and avoided death from snipers first received a mass of shells, and were then counter-attacked from all sides by an enemy "verminous with bombs." Our men were at first criticized for not consolidating as they went, for shirking the trench digging after the charge. The criticism had no grounds. The men never had a moment's leisure to use the spade, and they held every trench they reached till the last possible moment, perhaps too long. They had their crowded hour of glorious life, if men ever had; and the story of the sweep through "Devil's" Wood, and the push through Longueval village, which itself dovetails into that wood, will be ever memorable as a feat of arms in itself and as a triumphant sequel to a twelve days' battle. Our artillery went through the wood like a mower with his scythe: first one broad swathe, then a second at a certain remove, and, to conclude, a third, embracing the last of the wood.

The mowers moved like old-time harvesters and with as steady progression. But the cutting was rough, as of a crop that had been "laid" by wind and weather. The wood is thinner to sight than Mametz, but the floor of it all holes and humps. As the men moved on through the wood they met with little serious obstruction either from rifles, machine-guns, or bombs.

Prisoners surrendered; and our batteries had not fired more than a few rounds each when sixty Germans dashed from the wood with hands up. Even the Brandenburgers, of whose prowess the German accounts were afterwards full, gave themselves up, as they did before on the Aisne. I was surprised to find that one member of the Prussian Guard who was among the prisoners was of very small build. The fact was pointed out to other prisoners from the 102nd Saxons, but they refused to grant the grandeur of the Prussian. "Lots of the Berlin men are small like that," they said,

The enemy still left in the wood crouched in shell holes or very shallow trenches, making use of their time by devising methods of surrender - handkerchiefs tied to the end of entrenching tools to serve as a white flag, and, in one case, a Red Cross flag fixed to the end of a stretcher. Some men went on their knees, and "Kamerad, Kamerad" was heard from many men too frightened to show their heads or indicate the place of origin of their ventriloquial cry. One very small Tommy took captive a group of nine Germans collected in the crater made by a 12-inch howitzer or some such monster.

When the success of the attack was assured, and behind the third swathe our troops reached the edge of the wood, they saw the most cheering of all sights: groups of the enemy - in one case fourteen - running away up and over the hill, for the wood dips a little at its far edge. Some were in the open, some in communication trenches which we could enfilade with eye and rifle, some mere busts of men flying down trenches not more than three feet deep.

Doubtless the total of flying enemy thus seen was not large, but in a close war, a war of woods and trenches, the sight of enemy in open retreat is not often vouchsafed to infantry. They were, however, enough to keep the rifles busy. One sniper himself accounted for ten outside the wood.

The troops on the left advanced more slowly. On the village side the dugouts were many and deep. The orchard redoubt was not yet robbed of its thorns, and the enemy had a line of infiltration through the grove that juts out as a protective eaves over the north of the village. One of these dugouts had three openings, but each was filled up by our bursting shells, till one of our doctors scratched his way into it with a trenching tool, and that was later. Though the men in the wood were in advance of the men to right and left, and were a target for the enemy's artillery, they repelled during the afternoon two very furious and costly counter-attacks. Our own bombs and ammunition were passed forward with great speed, and the enemy's machine-guns and bombs were to some extent used against him. It was thought by several of the men engaged that the Germans had prepared their trenches with the definite idea of their recapture; that they had arranged and in some measure concealed stores - bombs, ammunition, and food - with the idea of being well and handily supplied when they retook the trench.

The attacks continued with persistence after bouts of heavy bombardment. Twice the enemy gathered some half-mile away and, moving through both communication trenches and through the long grass, drove a very heavy ram of men at our trenches north of the wood just east of the middle. A few got through into a section about 25 yards long, but all who reached that point were killed - some bayoneted, some bombed; and the losses were considerable both in the advance and the retreat. Some of our men told me that they found nothing so exhilarating as seeing the enemy gathering for a counter-attack. Like a good shot in the jungle - and the firing was good - they felt that the charging beast was dead the moment he faced the rifle.

Such moments had the Canadians known at Ypres in June - where one man sniped seventeen Germans - and the Australians round the Windmill off the Bapaume road. But the position was too hot to hold. We could not reinforce as the Germans could, and the men were in a salient. At one time the Germans, with no little skill and daring, rushed forward a field-gun on the right of the South Africans, fired it at point-blank range, and escaped untouched.

In every attack our thoughts are with the men in the front, face to face with the enemy; but there is a back part, and this the Germans sometimes treat as most worth attention. All through this fighting - and not least in the throes of this attack - they pelted the corridors of the advance with gas shells and tear shells, with 9% with 8-inch, with 5.9 howitzers, and with "universal" shrapnel from the 4.2. We had seen nothing much heavier since the war began.

The salient was no longer tenable. Men and munitions were too few, the lines of supply too difficult. So at last the remnant, after an incommensurable fight, were driven back to the nearer edge of the wood. There they were received by the Scottish, who would have passed them through to reserve positions. But they did not take the offer. They preferred to stay and pad out so far as might be the rather sparsely held position. The enemy came through the wood in multitude and with determination. They outflanked and overflowed the ends of our trenches, and all hopes of passive resistance were at an end. At this juncture two Scottish colonels met in a dugout and took counsel. They decided to "face it out, even to the edge of doom." Their method may be called "the bluff to the death." At a signal, the better part of the garrison leapt from the trench, and with a shout, as gay with the righting spirit as ever the clans heard, charged the advancing and marching enemy. The bluff did more than save the position. The Germans, altogether ignorant of the force upon them, and seeing only these ferocious and kilted soldiers rushing at their throats, fled incontinent. It was on the way back from this fight that an unwounded Highlander said to me, "They're no good when they see the whites of your eye."

Different companies, even different platoons, of the wood-fighters had very different experiences. One group of South Africans who had already borne the brunt of the righting, asked not to be relieved, and continued to fight without pause for six days and nights, during which few of them slept at all except while standing. Even when falling asleep as they stood, they repelled more than one furious counter-attack, firing and bombing with dash and accuracy. From this group one company became separated. As may easily happen in night-fighting in woods, they were lost by their companions. But they were not forgotten; nor should the tale of their struggle ever be forgotten.

How it all happened no one perhaps knew; but a hundred or so found themselves at twilight in occupation of a part of a trench running north and south up the wood. They could hear the enemy approaching both from east and west, and as he came up he began to throw bombs at a venture, hoping to flush his quarry; but, on instructions, not a man among the South Africans responded. Every man held his fire and waited till the figures of the enemy, now sure of their prey, were close and distinct. Then, attacking with rifle and bomb, they drove them back in panic and with heavy losses.

At one time some of the men in this single unsupported trench were facing and fighting both ways, some east and some west. A remnant of this lost garrison finally made good its retreat, joined hands with other troops, and with them renewed the attack.

Finally that happened at Delville which happened at Ginchy and Guillemont and at Trônes Wood. The nagging and costly struggle gave place to quick and triumphant assault. A tidal wave succeeded to the ebb and flow. Early in the morning as loud a tumult as ever man had heard broke all along the conquered slopes, and in it joined great guns lurking in forgotten places five and six miles away, opposite another front. Two hundred guns were directed on one part of the wood, which is in all no more than 200 acres, and they fired at the full limit of speed. It was the finish. The enemy could endure no more, though even so a machine-gunner or two - members of a picked and devoted band - waited for the assault. One German hereabouts was found tied to a post, and headless. The dead ground on this last occasion was a severer barrier than the enemy; and once again the worst came when the place was taken and held, and the enemy's guns could fire without fear.

For weeks afterwards you could read in the wood the proofs of Scottish and South African courage in a fight more grim than any glen or veld had ever known.

THE STORY OF HIGH WOOD

Tied up on the crown of the ridge almost in the middle of our line rests the diamond of High Wood. On 14th July a squadron of the Dragoons and the Deccan Horse galloped into the space behind it and tasted for a moment the joy of open battle. They were a little group; but their adventure brought into the history of war a new association of arms. As they galloped up the hill they were in danger of being exterminated by a machine-gunner ambushed in the corn. He was hidden from the ground, but not from the air. An airman had seen him and seen also the cavalry's danger. Never had cavalry a better ally. Hurrying to the rescue, the airman played the Pegasus indeed. He planed down to the rescue, fired his Lewis gun on the lurking gunner, and forced him to answer and declare himself. The cavalry once forewarned were forearmed. They rode down the gunner, and though a number of horses were lost they took prisoners, and afterwards deserting their proper work were of use to the tired infantry in digging trenches. That night we entered High Wood. We did not possess it till the afternoon of 15th September, just two months later, a long enough period to bring our miners into action and finally to give time for the approach of the secret and sluggish Tanks.

The wood might have been planted for defensive purposes. On the farther side it sloped rapidly down, offering a perfect artillery target from the north and altogether cutting off guns from the south, the northern end being protected by the southern trees which caught and exploded

126

even the highest angled shells. All these two months the wood nursed machine-gunners who kept all flanking attacks at bay.

Many troops made fame and suffered losses thereabouts, but the blazon of London regiments has the first claim to the decoration of the diamond Wood called High. One collection of London battalions had already fought to the death by Hébuterne on 1st July. Here another group won their spurs. If you would imagine the battle and know the mettle of the men, you must imagine the battle-field. I have seen nothing on earth like it: in desolation, in horror, in pitifulness, in fantasy, in grimness. At the west corner is a gigantic mine-crater lined and fringed with fragments of kit, with helmets and masks, and half-tunics and bones. An end of cloth protruding from a grave told you the regiment of the victim. The holes in the shrapnel helmet announced the nature of another death, and the stain on the boot a third man's anguish. Every tree is lanced and beheaded and maimed, while balked and unseasonable leaves put out from the scars in the trunks. At the very door of the wood a Tank lies lop-sided, careening in a shell hole with its nose thrust against the base of a tree growing from the far side. You walk through roots and pits and ditches that have supplanted the undergrowth; but there are worse things in the wood than the sights. No acres are so rich in noble dead. The wood - a smoking target for any and every battery - had been a field of battle for exactly two months. The Germans, who held the larger part, could not attempt to bury all their dead. It was difficult even for us. The enemy always held it strongly. The energy he put into its defence was more than Teutonic. Machine-gun emplacements were strengthened and multiplied daily. Iron girders and concrete blocks were brought up. Wiring was attempted quite close to our trenches. All the while an intense artillery fire was kept chasing up and down behind the wood and across it.

This fire redoubled on the eve of the great attack delivered on the morning of 15th September.

The Londoners, who bore the brunt of this, nevertheless went over the parapet as gaily as the rest. But they went of necessity more slowly. The wood was like nothing on earth when they faced it on that limpid dawn. Bits of men, bits of weapons, bits of trees lay tossed about and tangled together, some half buried, some suspended on stumps. The shells had gobbled in the undergrowth and among the roots like pigs in a full trough, and the sides, along which trenches ran, were little better than the wood proper.

The enemy, alert and in force at every turn, hidden in holes and trenches and behind -stumps of trees, was possessed of every machine and apparatus of defence. As the Londoners pushed forward, the gabble of machine-guns drowned even the artillery, but could never keep out of the ears the thin cries for stretcher-bearers nor smother the noisome reek.

The Tanks moved into the wood like obscene monsters; but even they could not face the music or thrid the maze. Only men could do that - men of breeding and intelligence, men bred and born in the soft work of the town. Office men, "daily-Dreaders," seekers after peace; only warlike from love of country and hatred of oppression. Their task seemed impossible; but they had great allies as well as their own great heart.

The hope of a quick attack lay in surprise, but there was no surprise; and it was impossible for our artillery to bombard the front trench held by the enemy. It was too near, and the trees would have caused premature explosions. When the hope was gone of steady progress in line with the troops on either side of the wood, the Londoners paused, retired a little way, and opened on the Germans with their own trench artillery, the mortars. These had been kept in abeyance in expectation that the Tanks and the suddenness of the dawn attack would do the work. But on this occasion the trench mortar was the surer method. The bombs, visible as birds topping the trees, went spinning up into the air, and the noise of the explosion drowned even the artillery. On the heels of the last salvos, so close to their own shells that some were wounded by the long ugly splinters, the Londoners scrambled through the maze, and at last found the enemy broken. They won by a direct frontal charge; but owed much to their friends on the flanks, especially the Northumberland Fusiliers, who surpassed that day even their own records. These Territorials had leapt into the open at dawn behind a very effective fire-curtain. Each trench they took and passed they found piled with dead. According to programme arranged with the artillery, they advanced in three bounds, stopping between each. The last took them to a shallow and ruined trench 900 yards beyond their first halt. At all times, when they moved or when they stopped, they were raked by machine-gun fire from the edges of the wood and sniped from every hole and corner. They crouched and scraped what holes they could, but never found any real protection, never had a moment's respite.

A friend of mine, engaged next the wood, lost more than half his unit. But they hung on hour after hour and found time to watch, with intense admiration, these valiant Londoners on their right struggling with the devilry in the wood.

For five hours the Northumbrians endured and the Londoners fought, gaining only by inches; but gaining nevertheless. At last the storm of trench mortars ended the desperation of the struggle. The weaker members of the enemy could endure no more; and at 11.20 - just five hours after the first onslaught - three hundred ran out and surrendered incontinent. A few minutes later several hundred more broke into the open, like pheasants at the end of a drive; and at last the Territorials outside had their revenge.

The fugitives were close to them. They opened on them with mortars, with bombs, with rifles, with machine-guns. If any man got away he was not seen to escape. The dead were like sheaves on the autumn stubble.

This reduction in the garrison of the wood made the work smoother for the Londoners. But the end was not yet. The toughest of the machine guns and a considerable number of infantry still held their ground, and in such a place one good man with a machine-gun may be as strong as a company. The end was not yet, but it was near. At one o'clock a very well-placed machine-gun near the point of the wood - the last to keep up its gabble - was struck by a heavy shell, and our soldiers clearly saw bits of the men and the machine rocketing into the air.

They knew now that they had won, and, fighting with vigour to the moment of the full finish, made their way through to the uttermost end. A harder, sterner, grimmer battle was never fought. No savage, no untutored men could have endured half what these Londoners or their friends suffered. Every child in London should feel himself higher in heart to be the fellow of such soldiers.

And it was a victory with high strategic results. The sequel was worthy. In the days that followed the enemy were sought in vain. Our patrols went forward and returned empty of all news. "Prue" Trench, beyond the wood, was empty. Men dug trenches peacefully and even sat out on the parapets. "It was like a rest camp," said one subaltern, " and it was quite hard to forbid the men to wander about hunting for souvenirs, everything seemed so peaceful."

No single event in the series of battles did more to break the enemy's confidence in himself than this joint combat in and round the peak of High Wood. The wood should be on London's escutcheon. When all was over those commanding inside and outside sent to each other messages of thanks and congratulation. Seldom had fellow fighters better cause for mutual admiration. Englishmen shook hands with Englishmen indeed. The last of the Somme woods was won.

CHAPTER X
THE VILLAGE

IT IS A sight most pitiful, and yet in spite of other feelings most fascinating, to see the destruction of a village by shell-fire. You watch it as you watch the crumbling away of a log in a wood fire, or the absorption of summer clouds into the invisible air, wondering idly at the permanence of certain bits and fragments and the rapidity of the dissolution of others.

I have seen many villages destroyed; but out of their combined ruin one single building will always stand supremely distinct. On 2nd July, while walking along the edge of a trench on my flowery hill behind the battle, I noticed a column of smoke rise from the midst of a fringe of trees on the opposite slope. Very soon the column was absorbed into other columns: the fire in the trees was spreading. Within twenty minutes the trees changed from summer to winter. They were leafless, as if a sudden frost had stripped them. Behind them now stood out a fine, rather pretentious house. It appeared "from the blue," in an almost stagey manner, as if the drop scene and curtain had been lifted, revealing the *mise en scène* of the true act. The house had two wings with pointed towers and a facade of broad windows. By the time all its features were plain the trees round and about it had been converted from a winter grove to a line of telegraph poles, so bare and boughless were they. All the while the house, the chateau of Contalmaison, remained miraculously intact, as to its frontal facade. Shells exploded at every spot in its neighbourhood, smothering it in smoke; but as the clouds blew aside, the twin towers reappeared, a rock unbroken by the surf.

For many hours of three days I watched the fortunes of that chateau with an insatiable, an almost morbid curiosity; and by some freak of luck, happened to be present at its most fateful hours. I had seen the very opening of the bombardment and the progressive wiping away of all surrounding features. On the third day, just as I topped the hill and turned with immediate curiosity towards Contalmaison, standing out in an atmosphere of visibility, such as we never enjoyed again during the battle, a most potent shell-burst appeared on the far side of the chateau. At the same moment a great piece of the left-hand tower collapsed. The impression was that the solid shell had hit it and exploded beyond. Such a thing happened to the church tower at Richebourg, bombarded in vain by the Germans, until a "dud" shell hit it in the centre and without help of explosion brought it clattering down. The chateau was now a skeleton. You could look through the hollow sockets of its eyes and observe, clearly with the naked eye, the broken bones of its limbs. But the skeleton remained still erect for a day or two; and until the Yorkshire men charged over the open into its shattered precincts the Germans were tending their wounded in the great cellars. A few days later one of the most moving pictures it has ever been my lot to see was drawn by our "official artist" Mr. Muirhead Bone, of this same Red Cross Station under British hands.

No village, except Combles, where many houses still stood for the fleeing Germans to ruin, has been taken while the houses stood. But there are degrees of destruction. Boiselle, which I did not detect as a village till I was at its edge, and then recognized not by houses but by a fringe of trees, only existed below the ground. Down among the fetid trenches through it you continually touched the foundations of houses. Above ground it was even flatter than Souchez, where the French fought one of the bitterest battles of the war. Through this the poor old padre, returning by moonlight to review the scene of his labours, passed and repassed without discovering the place where he had known every soul, every bush for years. "The place of it was no more seen." So it is with scores of villages; Guillemont perhaps is the worst of all. Just after one of our many assaults on this, I was present at a headquarters while the artillery attack was being discussed. It was decided to concentrate on a certain hundred yards along the south-western front a selection of every sort of heavy gun. One 15-inch, two 12-inch, and a number of 9.2 and 8-inch and 6-inch. This pack of "heavies" duly gave tongue and made good shooting. Even the dust and rubble of what had been houses vanished under their ministrations; and after an hour and a half our infantry advanced. Instantly, as soon as the first man was over the parapet, that hundred yards blazed with machine-guns. They rattled out as if all had been fired simultaneously by the pressure of a single electric contact.

Yet even so in the sequel, after several failures, after the total disappearance of two units, the Irish and Cornish and others of our light troops galloped through the rubbish, and a day later a photographer was taking pictures of an apparent field, really the site of the village, while another crossed beyond to trenches thick with German dead. They lay in one place propping one another up.

To one watching from a distance the attack on a village, there appears to be no room for human skill and courage among those colonnades of smoke and whorls of dust and that impenetrable reek. But character worked there and shone there as if every one had liberty of action. Seldom was any fight more productive of the characteristic virtue of different parts of the British Isles; of quiet, methodical English courage in "consolidating" in and "clearing up" - a very thankless task; and of Welshmen doing yeoman work as patrols (as they did long ago in their great advance through Mametz Wood), and not least of the Irish troops, who careered through the northern part of Guillemont.

Their triumphant rush through that village was curiously like the character of Irish football, though they dribbled no football as at Loos. Their "forwards" - who managed to get at the back of the chief German defences - charged with such impetus that everything but the zest of the rush was forgotten. They took no heed of machine-guns on the flank or even behind them, but cleared the village in their stride, went right across the open beyond, dived into the farther valley, where they concluded with some of the toughest fighting of the day along the sunken road.

Did I say "concluded"? Some groups were still insatiate, and mounted the slope almost to Leuze Wood, which was finally occupied two days later. How far they took their pipes with them does not appear; but they started their attack with the full blare of this intoxicating music. This charge was notable even in respect of the distance covered. It was an athletes', an Olympic charge, as well as a great feat of arms; and, before the end, a triumph of endurance. It gave a satisfying sense of the variety and association of talent in the new Army to picture these dashing Irish troops careering across the open, while the ground was being methodically cleared and settled behind them by English riflemen.

Indeed, the whole story of the capture of Guillemont was a model illustration of the Great Push in its later phase. Tactically perhaps the most important section of the battle was on the south-east, and not in the village itself. It consisted, in some part, of a duel of machine-guns, and yet further illustrated the development of this engine in the attack.

Our men, who were held up by well-placed guns of the enemy (some in a very deeply cut road, such as is common thereabouts), themselves brought up a score or so of guns, and once again beat the machine gun with the machine-gun. The Germans, proving very courageous, lifted theirs on to parapets and into shell holes. We did the same, finally getting the better of the duel; and in the sequel killing a number of fugitives. The whole field of this battle was thick with German dead, many of course previously killed by shell fire.

Guillemont and Ginchy were clean wiped off the face of the earth. Rather more was left of the villages stormed on 15th September, for they fell at the first assault. Among them Courcellette stands unique for the skill and surprise of its capture; and here a number of presentable houses fringed obvious and passable streets. The story is a wonderful one.

In the morning things had gone well. We had taken all the trenches attacked; we had occupied a mile or so of ground, along with several trenches and the sugar factory fort, where Tanks came to the rescue of the infantry who had outrun them. Within two hours a firm victory was won.

It was decided not to let well alone. All concerned came to the same decision. But the first step was taken by Ontario troops on the right.

With a promptitude that carried them almost - perhaps quite - into the arms of their own shell fire they pressed forward, leaving the village on their left, and most impertinently seized a reach of the sunken road that joins the sister villages of Martinpuich and Courcellette. They took prisoners, cleared dugouts, made firm in this most aggressive adventure, and remained almost alone all day with a vacant left flank. Germans appeared even behind them, and some groups came through them. Unruffled they continued to kill such rash intruders at intervals from 10.30 a.m. to 6 p.m., when the greater adventure began on their left.

The splendid isolation of this wing was not to endure through the night. Great preparations had been made in the afternoon by troops in the rear. Right across the open, as in wars of movement before trenches were in fashion and shrapnel universal, strong supports had formed up and deployed this way and that with ingenious strategy. In the desolate landscape they had little but a compass to guide them. A chimney and house they were to steer by had already fallen to high explosive. Straight in front of them a German kite balloon swung with obvious malevolence, endowed with the eyes of Argus and the wings of Mercury. Its messages had already reached the German artillery, as anyone could infer.

The commander of one of the regiments which were to have the centre of the fight himself was buried three times, one of his officers told me. He moved like a shuttle, this way and that, himself continually correcting in person the alignment of the men and giving them their direction. "It was nothing. I just had to shake the earth off," was his own version. So they advanced, mile after mile, and just reached the leaping-board at the due moment.

The morning charge was at 6.20 - the dawn of the anniversary of the arrival of these Canadian troops in France. It was nobly celebrated. The evening charge was just twelve hours later. Again all went pat. The barrage, the promiscuous bombardment, were nicely calculated. The filtering of the infantry into positions at an angle with their line of march - a "left incline" complicated by trenches - went smoothly; and at the ordered moment the lines swept forward on to Courcellette.

It was strongly garrisoned. Two regiments had their headquarters, well stocked and well equipped, in neighbouring cellars. At this moment their commanders were snugly housed there, and scattered about the village were about 1200 of their men - Prussians of the proudest sort. But they hardly played a soldier's part that evening. The French Canadians, who took more than half of the village, went through them like a pike through minnows. A few stopped to be bayoneted, a few tried to use machine-guns, but the mass retired or dived well underground till they were hidden by platoons in a cave.

New Brunswickers followed on the heels of their companions to sweep the place clean. Their only trouble was to find the holes. These were often small, half covered with rubbish, and sometimes ingeniously disguised. The "sweepers," who played as difficult and dangerous a game as the rest, came provided with bombs and other apparatus of the trade; but they had little use for them. The rabbits did not wait for the ferrets. A frightened mask appeared at one orifice. "I'll give you two minutes to bring all the out," said a little Canadian then acting as "runner"; and within two minutes - quite safely within two minutes - twenty-seven German soldiers, each with his hands up like an Egyptian idol, stumbled out. If a man put a hand to steady himself he brought it back instantly to the surrender position with a nervous click. Between 600 and 700 men were so collected. It was "as easy as shelling peas," this capture of the village, and filled our men with a surprising contempt of their enemy.

The fight had only just begun, nevertheless. The evening was the eve of a more heroic wrestle. The village was captured, but the enemy was firmly placed in a strong system of deep trenches just outside the pale, beyond the quarry and the cemetery. He had an admirable base for a counter stroke and good opportunity for one of the night attacks that he loves.

In the darkest hour of a night never very dark, bombs, grenades, and other bursting things began to fall in and round the quarry. They increased in number and were lobbed from nearer and nearer. Just as a company commander was making last arrangements for defence a group of four men, maddened by battle-field fury, drunk with the confidence born of this day's fighting that the Germans could never stand the sight of cold steel - these four, yelling like wild Indians, left the cover of the quarry for the open. The noise of the shout and the bursting bombs forced an answering halloo from the rest of our men.

The bombs suddenly ceased. Lights, fired up in quantity from the stores left behind by the enemy, disclosed the hinder parts of many green-coats stumbling away in this direction and that, for he was attacking as usual in little groups moving from different parts. At many times in these three days from Friday night to Sunday night the German was to be hit behind. In the earlier advance men had knelt down to rest the elbow on the knee for the surer sharpshooting of the fugitives. Later they were shot by their own weapons. We found in the trenches many rifles with much ammunition; and very valuable they proved, serving well at a crisis, saving much carrying up of extra rounds.

In a more positive way, too, the enemy helped us. Among the prisoners were two doctors; and if any class in Germany is to be acquitted of blood-guiltiness it is the medical. All day and night they worked whole-heartedly. "We have nothing to do with the war but to help wounded men," they said, and they kept to their creed faithfully in the dugout wards of Courcellette.

A strange experience in the capture of prisoners was that of an officer who was left badly wounded in a trench, refusing to keep anyone else back from the fight. As he lay there four Germans slowly emerged from a dugout almost at his feet. He covered them with his revolver, forced them to throw down their weapons, instructed them in the art of botching a temporary stretcher, and finally persuaded them to carry him back to a distant dressing-station.

A stranger experience yet befell two unwounded officers. During a furious barrage they took refuge in a shell hole and began digging themselves a shelf. "Did you feel something move?" said one. "Dig on and mind nothing else," said the other. Presently the heaving below them became more palpable and persistent, and further delving into the floor of their nook revealed a dead German whose body heaved up and down. They exhumed the corpse and disclosed below it the head and shoulders of another German apparently quite unhurt. Him they cleared to the middle, provided with a trenching tool to undig his lower limbs, and finally left with instructions to cut a trench between this shell hole and the next. And, like a good German, he did what he was bid. He undug himself.

In this fight, as in all fights, "touches of things human" rose to "touch the spheres." On the body of a German officer lying stone dead and supine sat a small dog, "as near crying as a dog can go." Now and again he licked the dead face and whined in a whisper. He refused food and could not be made to leave. Two days before I had seen one of our own Guardsmen's dogs as full of grief and as far beyond consolation. Tactically, humanly, every way, this fight for Courcellette stands out. A single company took at least five hundred prisoners. An important trench in front of the village the day after its capture was charged and taken by no more than twenty-five French Canadians. A single man went out, took a machine-gun, carried it back, and offered to get "ever so many more."

And the best parts of the story cannot yet be told. For myself, I see through all of it the figure of one man, the ideal officer that such issues always call up. He was in the Guards' attack too, marching, directing, acting as his own runner, making great decisions, sleepless, vigilant, quiet, incredibly active, hopeful against hope, eager to do or die, alert for either issue. When the Germans break his line he begins to realize that "things are not looking very bright." When they run he thanks God for his fine troops. He bears a charmed life, and his men feel too certainly for any misgiving that the German will run from their bayonets, whatever the odds; and suppose he does not, the hopeful men fight the better.

A man indeed is needed for such war. These troops advanced nearly three miles under the enemy's eyes in heavy shell fire. They stormed a fortified place strongly held, made good their ground, and fought continuously for two more days, repelling seven counter-attacks. All the while, before and after the advance, shells descended round them without intermission.

No village perhaps has any unchallenged preeminence in the length of its siege or the degrees of its collapse. To-day not one exists at all to outward view: Montauban, Fricourt, Mametz, Guillemont, Ginchy, Flers, Gueudecourt, Morval, Le Sars, Martinpuich, Courcellette, Boiselle, Ovillers, Pozières, Thièpval, St. Pierre Divion, Beaucourt, Beaumont-Hamel. Most of them you cannot see till you enter. Ovillers we won yard by yard in hand-to-hand fighting that never ceased day and night. In Pozières the houses by the road were so long bombarded that a continuous riband of some breadth was shrivelled by successive shells into fine dust scattered over miles of country. British shells destroyed the village, but none of our shell holes remain. They were soon ploughed out and crossploughed and harrowed by successive barrages of 5.9, working with monotonous persistence week after week. The villages which we left in partial ruin, such as Le Sars and Courcellette, the German continues to finish off, and will while he can reach.

Half these villages deserve the fame of Badajoz, and evoked as high courage - historic spots all; but if they have a crown, the crown is Thièpval. It was the master bastion of the German defence. The French told us we should never take it. The face of the hill leading to it was a warren of strong places, with the Wonder Work in the middle, an oval of trenches, redoubts, and dugouts, where you could watch our shells exploding day in, day out. Below it was the Leipsic Redoubt, the one corner of trenches hereabouts taken on 1st July. Alongside this was Mystery Corner, a harmless-seeming angle of German territory, of which our patrols were not fond. Men who crossed it were assaulted by unseen men from unknown directions, arising, as was afterwards seen, from many-holed dugouts.

All this land was curiously visible. You could go close to it. You could watch the very effect of separate shells and keep record of the progressive whittling away of the apple trees that fringed the near face, Within Thièpval we knew that a picked regiment of Wurtembergers had lived for twenty months or so. They had fortified the place and made it so cosy that they obtained leave to stay there, as at home, working their own reliefs, as a self sufficing unit.

The place was as nearly as may be impregnable. But slowly we closed in. Three brilliant little rushes at different dates took us up to the Wonder Works and beyond. Troops closed in from the east, though the ridge of the hill was so thorny that no one dare stay in force along certain trenches. The doom of Thièpval approached. It fell on the morning of 23rd September - at the first assault, though the fighting was furious - almost coincidently with Combles, that bigger village in the hollow of the hills at the other end of the line. Its capture - in which Middlesex troops played a most gallant part - did more to enhance the glory of the British army in France than any other single event. I had seen many advances against Thièpval, but the day of its capture had walked with an officer to catch a near glimpse of Combles. As we reached a turn in the road in the shattered village of Maurepas we met a very tired but very eager French brigadier who had led his men into Combles and taken the biggest group of prisoners. He sat on a rickety chair by the roadside, utterly wearied by want of sleep and much movement, but was already on his way to organize a new advance. His eyes glinted with excitement as he saw the khaki. "Is it true about Thièpval?" he asked; and when we said it was true, felicitations poured forth in a stream in which every other word meant glorious. Then he told us his story, and sent us on our way to watch from close quarters the baffled Germans sullenly pounding the relic walls and filling the air with a red dust, as if the light of sunset were on the cloud.

CHAPTER XI
THE OPEN FIELD

A NEW WORLD seemed to be disclosed when the last of the woods on the battle-field fell into our hands; for it stood on the peak of the ridge. You could see a new world, a free, natural world, with cultivated fields below, and the homely-looking clock tower of Bapaume, and the tall spire of Pys church and the old historic monument - soon to be called "the Gunner's Delight" - known as the Butte of Warlencourt. Even the signs of war were diminished. Fewer trenches and less wire were visible from High Wood, and for a while even artillery fire languished.

The war appeared at last to be open. More than ever our men avoided trenches. A large notice, "Use the trench here," was at first entirely disobeyed by five or six pioneers hurrying forward for their night work in No Man's Land close to High Wood, though presently they were driven to cover by a shell. Generally one felt a coward if one hugged a trench closely. Such was the sentiment of the new field; but the deception of semblance seldom went further. Below the smooth lava crust the fires burned. The new warfare nursed terrors of which even the woods were innocent.

From the first few days of the Somme battle soldiers began to acquire the new habit of moving in the open. The valleys and hill-sides seethed with activity. Horses were corralled everywhere. Avenues of horses pencilled out the valleys. You smelt horse wherever you wandered. At one only reach of a little stream that I passed almost daily forty-eight thousand horses watered within each twenty-four hours. These were just within shell fire.

Nearer the line men took the place of horses; and at first it was difficult to believe the eyes when you saw the troops scattered all over the slope, without any apparent attempt at concealment, as if artillery fire did not exist. And yet the shells from our own guns almost scraped the heads of some of these groups, and they moved in a world of perpetual clamour. The limit of this freedom of movement was reached on 16th September, when the enemy hurried down the slope.

Such freedom could not last long, and did not. The very worst of the war was to come, and a new guerrilla warfare began to emerge. You may tear heart out of comparison and find no simile to convey a picture of the open battle-field. Imagine the carpet of snow under a tree when the thaw begins and dibbles every inch with dirty holes and put the picture under a microscope; further, imagine the surface littered with dirty fragments of all sorts of cloth and metal and of live things - so you may gather some perception of the surface of the battle-field. Up beyond Pozières where shelling was perhaps thickest, shell cases lay so close that you could scarcely avoid trampling them in. Some were collected to serve as metal for a light railway, but the number was not sensibly diminished thereby. Along certain strips the shells had so continued to churn the soil that its particles were attenuated to dust which agglutinated into mud as prehensile as glue - a chemical compound beyond the power of manufactury. Across the most easterly slope round the village of Lesbœufs the effect of the dibbling was to rob the landscape of any distinction. It was difficult beyond belief to discover even approximately which line of earth corresponded to the map-line, and the whereabouts of the enemy was as shrewd a problem.

So the new guerrilla war came to develop. Any hole anywhere might conceal a sniper or a machine gunner. A regular system was worked out by the enemy for converting the hole into a redoubt. The gunner tunnelled a deep hole for himself into which he could slip when the shells began, without leaving his gun for more than a second or two at a time; and for the gun itself a little square earth-walled redoubt was contrived. Positions were no longer held by trenches, but by scattered fortresses, isolated strong points, irregular butts, eccentric ambuscades. The artillery were robbed of the regular target offered by a trench and a properly engrooved enemy, and could only spray the surface of the ground and sweep it back and fore.

Across all that archipelago of holes separating the villages of Morval and Lesbœufs and Le Transloy we saw day after day, first shrapnel and then high explosive, or shrapnel close on the heels of high explosive, searching out these death-traps; and now and again bits of gun or woodwork or man would swivel round into the air, a solid object in the midst of the dust and mud and smoke, the eruption of a 9.2 shell. The men fighting in this open country, not in woods or villages, engaged in battles without definition; and sometimes lost the glory, the reputation that belongs to a victory with a habitation and name. In some degree the Guards so suffered. They came up into the line for the battle of 15th September: Grenadiers, Coldstreamers, Scotch, Irish, and Welsh Guards. It was almost a battle to get into the line, from the zigzag of trenches merging into shell holes above the ruins of Ginchy. No one, not even the airman and map makers, could quite give them the chart either of their own trenches or of the lines they were to take. As they discussed the great fight to come and the weapons and stores they would need, a young officer said, "What we shall want most is our compasses"; and he himself afterwards earned fame and a decoration by the coolness with which he stood on the stricken field and took bearings with map and instruments.

Ugly and formless was the country, and will be for many days, perhaps years. But when we hear or read the names of the gallant men who fought and died in it, we should have some picture in our mind of what they faced and endured for home and country. Many whose names are known through the length and breadth of the land perished in this chaos. Raymond Asquith, a fine soldier and a gallant spirit, was one among the losses of the Grenadiers, who fought throughout, with an exposed flank and under artillery observation. Never was a more gallant fight recorded, in a field so foully featured and void.:

Here for the first time in history three battalions of the Coldstream Guards went over in line. They were swept and raked by rifle and machine-gun fire from many directions, and all the while the shells fell right and left. For 200 yards the blast in their front and flank was enough to have stopped a locomotive. It did not stop the men. In the midst of it, of a sudden they came upon an unsuspected trench from which the enemy rose in thick ranks. The sight was all they needed to add the last touch to their fighting spirit. At last they were at grips, man to man, when the better man would win.

The enemy fired rifles point blank and threw bombs. The Guards used only the bayonet. Each man, they said, got his man. The enemy fought now in the open as well as below ground, and the sight of these new regiments, body to body, hand to hand, stabbing, hitting, even wrestling, so stirred the Irishmen coming up in support that they rushed forward at the double to take their part. Men, N.C.O's, subalterns, commanding officers, doctors, artillery observers, burst into an incredible shout, smothered by the noise of the guns, but like the swish of the shells savagely inspiriting.

The enemy had fought well. He thought he could stop the Guards; but the bayonet was irresistible, and of a sudden the desperation of the struggle broke. "We flushed 'em and they rose like a covey of partridges." The battle became a chase. The prisoners who surrendered were just given leave to hurry back without escort to our lines, and took the permission at the gallop, to be rounded up like homing sheep, away behind. One group went astray, headed off in its nervousness by other advancing troops, before it was again corralled off like any other half -wild animal. The fight and the chase went on, morning, day and evening. Germans rose from mysterious holes and picked off isolated men. One Guardsman had a duel at 60 yards with a Bavarian sniper. Each fired three shots. The Guardsman's last went home and the German fell.

All this while, whether advancing or stopping in shell holes or trenches, officers greeted one another as if they were meeting in Piccadilly, with familiar greetings and Christian names and the common chaff of the regiments. Unimaginable events made little difference. A young subaltern, in battle for the first time, was transferred of a sudden "into a maze of glory," conscious that he was dead, that was all. Presently he found himself at the bottom of a shell hole quite unhurt, when he continued his mission of search for a machine gun officer. He met one at last and asked him his name. He asked once, twice, three times, without eliciting an answer. At last the man put his mouth to his ear, made a

144

funnel with his hands, and bellowed his loudest. Then for the first time the subaltern understood that the shell which had opened the earth beneath him had left him stone deaf. But the deafness, too, passed. He fought all day, and spent the night at patrol work making posts in front of the line.

Some golden moments were vouchsafed in this immortal charge, which carried the Guards over a mile and more of shell-raked and bullet-raked desert. While they drove the Germans before them the sun, below the horizon when they started, had reached high noon. It lit a new landscape. A German battery was seen in action, the officers taking notes and the gunners shovelling shells into the breech. Enemy's transport trailed along the roads. Undamaged steeples rose from the midst of peaceful villages. But soon the panorama shifted like "the baseless fabric of a vision." The German guns limbered up and galloped off. The transport vanished, and just a little while later the village houses toppled and the homesteads merged into the general desolation of war.

Some figures emerge from the ruck of battle in almost ghostly salience. An officer who felt then and afterwards that he had never lived so splendid, so exhilarating a day in his life - such men do really exist - took no cover, but went exultingly forward to any nucleus of resistance he could discover. He killed man after man, some with the pistol, some with a stick.

One of his men, as great an athlete, if less endowed with valkyrie spirit, rushed a machine-gun post, shot two of the men, bayoneted a third, and "caught the fourth a clip with my fist." Some rival of another company then claimed the captive machine-gun; but the Irishman settled the dispute by taking the weighty thing under his arm and carrying it back deliberately across the open. He did not stop till he had delivered it personally to the headquarters of his unit. While officers greeted one another with the natural exchange of social phrase, the men called out hilarious encouragement: "Go it, Lilly whites," "Go it, Ribs" using the vocatives of the playing field. And here it was, out in the open, that Colonel Campbell blew a Roland and Oliver blast on his silver hunting-horn and rallied his Coldstreamers to the final triumphant charge, as he would call his harriers over Shropshire fields. The day after the fight I saw men stroke that horn and touch it as if there were health and honour in the mere contact. But all day and night it was bitter fighting, as every man and every officer knew.

The enemy ran, but it was not allowed to pursue them. I heard an officer apologize to his men, almost with tears, because he had forbidden longer pursuit. Trenches occupied were often shallow and very full - full of Germans, some gibbering, some obsequious, some wounded and crying for food or water, some quite quiet; full, too, of fighters, some hale, some dead, some wounded. The padre was all day in the front line giving religious consolation where he could, and at night helping to bury the dead. Stretcher-bearers tried to push up, and when unable went into the open without fuss or hurry. Shells fell all the while - big shells and some mysterious shells smaller than the 3-inch. Wounded men were taken into the small but deep dugouts that the enemy had dug in this loamy soil. In some both doctors and padres found hiding Germans and sent them hustling off to the rear.

Through it all order reigned, though companies were mixed together; and one bit of trench might be crammed while another was neglected. In spite of all this crumples were . smoothed out. Officers with compasses and surveying tools quietly took bearings, and orderlies were sent back with precise messages. Our artillery battered a counterattack and sent a German battalion scattering till it vanished like steam from an engine. Patrols went forward. Good digging was done. Water and food were brought up, and here and there astonishing supplies of soda-water, bread, and coffee beans collected in German dugouts.

The history of the Guards contains no finer record. "It was worth living, even if I am killed to-morrow, just to have seen such men charge," said one commanding officer, whose speech to his men after action will be remembered lifelong, almost syllable by syllable, by all who heard it. Nor in war at any time is any scene more moving than when, the battle over, a regiment lines up under some shelter in the misty dawn to take toll of the missing. However gaily men fight, at that moment they love not war. And the Guards fought the gayest fight of which ever I heard news or any troubadour dreamed; and fought it against bitter odds, the odds of an open flank; and won, inflicting more than they suffered.

In this attack by the Guards, the base of attack was a regular trench, and the first enemy they met were in regular trenches; but both here and yet more on the highland beyond the Windmill off the Bapaume road ground was sometimes held solely by posts, as in the early days of the war. The worst of the enemy's artillery fire was thus avoided; but such a post needs more nerve and common sense in the garrison than any trench. It is a task in itself, when dusk comes, to separate friend from foe. Even if a bomb falls it does not follow that one of your own patrols have not thrown it. The posts are difficult to relieve, partly because they are difficult to find; and not a few men have been lost.

The use of the shell hole encouraged night-fighting. Indeed, latterly the enemy became a night bird, as ill-omened as any owl. His artillery and his scattered machine-guns both doubled activity after dusk fell. Across the open, above Pozières, Germans lay about in shell holes as snug as trap-spiders or hermit-crabs; but he trusted for his safety wholly to utter secrecy by day and to darkness by night. While the sun was up these lurkers fired no single shot; but at night the rattle of their machines was as continual as, often, it was vain. So easy was it to mistake your fears for a figure, and to imagine an attack every time a star-shell hung for a moment in the air.

Of course the shell hole and the trench merged imperceptibly one into the other. A trench much shelled might be less like a trench than a line of accidentally symmetric shell holes on the flat. Indeed, we once mistook such a line for a trench, and were amazed to find no Germans in possession. And the shell holes were more easily welded into a trench than the damaged trench itself. But it may be said that at many points the shell hole has become a real rival to the sap, the fire, the front, support, assembly, communication, or any and every other sort of trench. Such now is the standard method of fighting.

Half the latest trenches are little more than shell holes linked up. By their means a makeshift line may be constructed in a few hours, as we proved and the enemy proved again and again. Defences spring up like mushrooms in the course of the night, and the attacking force has no well defined obstacle to face. Often you cannot say where one line begins and the other ends, for No Man's Land has developed into Every Man's Land, and swelled in size beyond all recognition.

A strange and grim warfare is this. Men have become like wild beasts in the jungle, some trusting for safety to stillness in their forms or lairs, some prowling and alert to spring. The wounded may be lying at the bottom of these treacherous holes, and the life-savers may sometimes lose their lives in vain searchings. In a night attack by Bazentin le Petit a Midland soldier, from a company who had lost direction for the moment, rushed forward with his county's name as a battlecry to prove whether he and his were approaching friend or foe, and he fell wounded by a friend's bullet. You could find no finer heroism than that, no higher sacrifice, nor any more pitiable example of the blind muddle of war.

Over the middle and centre of our line we had always the better of the German at this guerrilla warfare in the archipelago of shell holes; but he held us up for a month in the spaces in front of Le Transloy on the right more by virtue of the isolated sharpshooter than by such strong points and redoubts as the Stuff and Schwaben mud fortresses which we stormed on the hill above the Ancre. Vague lines of country, marked by sunken roads and old gun emplacements and howitzer holes tidied up, were taken and retaken five or six times; and when all was over no one quite knew where anyone else was. To such a state has the heavy shell and the science of the new warfare reduced what should be open fighting.

Some attempts were made to take advantage of the open held and the open fight, to pretend it was really open. When we were approaching Le Sars pn the 1st of October, a few horsemen strayed into the half-empty land away on their left; and one of them brought back a story of knight-errantry that leaves chronicles of the Middle Ages bankrupt. Even robbed of its more picturesque details it is curious enough.

A pair of knights smuggled their horses up in the dusk and rode out, seeing no enemy, till at length both their steeds were shot from some subterranean ambush or other. Undeterred, the two proceeded on foot. Presently they saw a white flag waved by an unseen hand, but as they approached the place, a flanking enemy fired from a neighbouring hollow, and one knight fell. The other, serpentining his way through the muddy labyrinth, entered the ambush and took two Germans prisoners. He returned with the captives to his base trench and again set forth, meeting similar adventures, and again started home, this time with a major as his captive, joining a Red Cross cavalcade on the way. All went well till a great shell scattered the whole party. The knight-errant found himself still unharmed, but his captive had clean vanished, perhaps into thin air.

Such adventures may seem incredible even to men righting in the neighbourhood, but the tale is no more than a sober epitome of what really happened on a quiet autumn afternoon near the French hamlet of Pys. And it is no exception. The patrol work all through the righting was compact of adventurous surprises.

But it was not till October came that the enemy quite developed his "open-air system" of defence, when day after day of rain and diminishing hours of evaporation made marshland of the hill-sides, when horses bringing ammunition sank to their hocks, when men crawled from their trenches on all fours, when the straggler ran real risk of drowning and the walls of trenches subsided by their own weight and weakness, when brigadiers, colonels, and majors as well as the rest were sniped as they deviated across the open, avoiding the communication trench as an evil worse than the risk of death.

When we give thanks for brave soldiery, when we recall the travail they have endured in battle and between whiles, when we try to picture the pains and penalties of the men in the trenches, we should think perhaps first of the men who fought in October and November, when the Somme battle was near its finish, in the shallow, unrevetted trenches stretching between the flattened villages. Every one knows how gloriously the Australians fought at Pozières when they stormed it. Few know what grim days they spent in the glue of the trenches between Gueudecourt and the Butte. Bitter rights were fought here as in front of Le Transloy by English troops, of which nothing has been heard or will be heard, so muddy and obscure and ill defined was the nature of each engagement and each period of the day's work. Reliefs spent a day in reaching their destination. Supplies of food and wire and ammunition could scarcely be got through at all. When an attack was attempted the shells buried themselves without exploding, and the men were literally ensnared by the mud, so that they could neither advance nor retreat nor fight where they were. Captured prisoners could scarcely be extracted. Shells, which did not kill, buried, and scores of heroic rescues were to the credit of pioneers and other soldiers, who spent two, even three, hours in digging out a single man smothered in one of these earth slides.

The Slough of Despond never equalled some marshes in this righting area; and yet the men bore it out without any surrender or weakening of their will to conquer. They "stuck it." They "carried on."

CHAPTER XII
COMING OUT

I F YOU WISH to feel the full humanity of a tale of battle hear and see the men who have fought through it all the very day after they have left the field. Earlier is too early; for as they come back into billets or camp they are one and all weighted down with sleep. You wonder sometimes whether they will tumble down with the burden, though they walk briskly and sing in snatches.

One of the bitterer battles by Pozières lasted, for a unit on which my personal interest was centred, a whole six days. A brigadier-general had slept just one and a half hour in the six days. One of the soldiers had slept not at all for four days; but except for a shrapnel hole in his helmet and a shrapnel scratch on the lip, showed small sign of the fighting in person or in kit. He was setting off quite cheerily on a three hours' walk.

One begins to believe that the power or will to do without sleep is the greatest of all battle-winning gifts or forms of courage. To murder sleep is certainly one of the aims of modern tactics. One company in this battle fought eight long and distinct bomb-fights up German trenches subsequent to the first charge. The enemy was using almost exclusively his newer little and light bombs, each about the size of an egg. We replied with our bigger and more dangerous bomb, and the struggle oscillated up and down two parallel trenches almost continuously day and night.

But it is less the active labour than the length of the fighting hours which tells. Usually the men can be relieved within forty-eight hours, and that is long enough for any troops if the action has been hot; but in some of the rough-and-tumble trench fights, where no clear objective is marked, a battalion, or, at any rate, a platoon or two may be entangled in a limitless struggle. At any time the arrival of the relief is one of the greatest events; and no man is more genuinely hated for the moment than the relief which is late. In the old days of stagnant trench warfare, when the front trenches were a sort of home, where food could be cooked in almost luxury, and the road of departure up a revetted alley was safe and sound, the hour of relief mattered less, though it mattered much. At the worst time in the Ypres trenches, a Guardsman of catering genius boasted, "We always had five courses and a glass of port to finish with," even in the front line. But when the trench is unstable mud, a line marked on no map, or, if marked, bumped out of all shape, when the alley or avenue does not exist, for the trench has just been captured, when food and drink have come up in the meagrest driblets, if at all, when every nerve has been racked by the sights and sounds of open battle, of friends killed and beyond recognition, of others calling faintly for help - then the lateness of the relief is a tragedy. You await them in an agony. Even the most patient or insensate find the tension extreme. An hour or two more or less of endurance could be easily suffered, as part of the day's work, if a race were not involved, the race with dawn. If the relief does not come "good and early" the silhouettes of the outgoing troops will be visible to enemy observers; and men who have just won and lived through a face-to-face fight will be shot in the back as they slip away.

The Guards had one unendurable experience of this sort after their first great fight. One of them - a man of letters - caught himself murmuring again and again, "Risest thou thus, dim dawn, again?" as he watched the light struggling over that void and shapeless ridge while the belated relief slowly and deliberately "took over." His anxiety exceeded all fears in the battle itself; and he had suffered much, rounding up a day of death and wounds with patrol work at night away in front of the trench. When at last he and the others slipped away, each felt inordinately visible till he was over the ridge and drew up under the ridge to count losses, to tabulate cold facts of dead and wounded, to be assured of the number of the men with whom he would never mess again.

A few days later some Northumberland Fusiliers suffered yet worse things. The relief, half bogged in the mud, took nine hours to make the journey, and arrived when dawn had broken. Double forces held the trench through the day, and when night came these half-exhausted men started themselves on an infinite march: five hours along the pock-marked slope, three more along the alleged road, another hour and a half to reach the rough little village where they might at last bed down in some sort of ease, if not comfort. Not often is the demand on cheerfulness and stamina so exacting as this; for not often is the weather so wet, the ground so sodden, the alley so tumbled. But always a man needs an athlete's training and an Englishman's spirit to come through the ordeal as a veteran soldier should. It is hardest when the time in the trench was itself a mere act of endurance, a suffering of cold and wet and shell-fire. After a victory the men will sing and jest through any trial, even though the march comes at the end of a week of hard fighting and slow endurance of desperate shelling. When such troops come away from the field thinned in ranks, licking their wounds, as I met them after the capture of Guillemont, worn in body and mind, less this officer and that companion; when the general, with mixed tears of pride in his voice, says to them as they pass, "Well done, men, well done!" when they march on in companies no bigger than platoons, scarcely able to know whether their victory or loss weighed most - a man who has not faced the music with them can hardly endure to write of the glory of victory.

The press and tumult of war are on every side. Cannon and caisson and van and lorry and marching troops and teams of horses and mules, and above all the still unceasing clamour of innumerable guns and bursting shells, make such a setting for the return of the fighters that only war values count and are reckoned. It is war to the death. The fight they came from, the great and crucial victory they won had all of war in it. They fought in the open; they stormed strong places like citadels; they captured prisoners; they dug defences; they used machine-guns, rifles, bombs, grenades, bayonets; and the wounds were received and given by almost every engine,, chemical or mechanical, known in modern war.

Yet all this is put aside from the minds of most of the men as they come near the end of the march. Billets are a more crucial question than bullets. Even souvenirs (the helmets they vaunt and - perhaps - the gewgaws they conceal) yield to the thought of sleep and food, but first and foremost of sleep - sleep anywhere, in mud-barn or dilapidated cellar. If you told them that the impossible was to happen, and they were to sleep in beds, they could hardly look more contented.

Spirits recover long before the battalion is out of the range of shells. After a desperate and muddy fight beyond Pozières, some Kentish and other south county troops entertained some of us in a tent pitched on a spot round which the enemy was peculiarly fond of distributing odd shells, big and small. The men had not yet made good any of the arrears of sleep and rest; but their sense of humour and gaiety was so restored that from their tale you would have thought that the battle was a jest. These Kentish troops had begun the attack "in a smell of rotten eggs," as they said, or the fumes of many score shells of asphyxiating gas. They had been pelted with bombs. The German bombers, freed from all trappings, stood in front of trays covered with bombs, which they picked up and threw almost as smartly as a printer picks up type.

The English were raked by machine-guns from both right and left. They passed through curtains of condensed fire. They had hammered and been hammered for two or three days unceasingly, but to listen to their tale of the righting was to split your sides with laughter; and no narrator was more humorous than that soldier who had fought continuously since Mons and suffered all the terror of those munition less winter and spring months in Flanders without loss of high spirits. There was a fortune for a music-hall star in the account of the German prisoner, laden with heavy kit, and so nervous when ordered to doff it that he could scarcely distinguish between his rifle, his straps, and his bombs.

The story of the bolting of Germans from a crowded dugout was Rabelaisian. Imagine a single soldier in a strange trench at night-time controlling a crowded cave of foreign-speaking enemy! Sometimes he shouted instructions; sometimes he listened, as a keeper listens at a rabbit -hole, - the comparison is the soldier's, - and heard rumblings and patterings which indicated that some of the occupants were making for the bolt-hole. To this he had to run like a fussed terrier, to stop them bolting too quick or persuade them to bring out the wounded first.

The most delightful incident of all was the final marshalling and marching off of one large group of prisoners. The soldiers told off to conduct them were so pleased and proud of their job that they marched off with fixed bayonets *at the head of the procession*, with the whole queue of Germans behind them, and this at night!

What human, pitiful, contradictory feelings and episodes stand out in sudden distinctness from such a night! A subaltern, full of fight, half savage for the time and in a mental ecstasy, rushes to stab a Prussian soldier. The glint of a Verey light catches the German's face, and a sudden pity intervenes. He seizes the enemy by the belt and throws him behind him. As he falls, his whole person rattles and the subaltern sees that the German's belt is festooned with bombs at which he is fingering. Imagine how one of those eighty soldiers of the nth Prussians whom the Kents took prisoner, would have told the story! How full it would have been of blood and death and terror and glory and the hated foe!

Billet scenes are as vivid in many minds as battle scenes. Sometimes the troops retire directly into tents, and there are camps more famous or notorious than any groups of houses or dugouts; but the most constant picture of hours of relief from the Somme fighting is of one particular type of village. Along the streets, churned into permanent mud by war traffic, run not for the most part houses and cottages, but barns and outhouses built of lathes and mud, a substance that needs, but in war-time hardly receives, regular repair. Behind these rather forbidding stables is concealed a courtyard, often used as a manure dump; and behind that a comely little house or cottage.

How often have I passed through the kitchen, where an old man and woman of all ages sit down to lap their midday soup, and opened the inner door into the officer's mess-room. The cleanliness, the polish set on things, depend very much on the interval between the arriving and the departing guest, for men follow close on one another's heels, or those coming back from the line may pass almost at the door those going forward; and many of these billets are only occupied for one or two nights. I should doubt if any event on the battlefield, however tragic, produces so fine a flow of complaint as the sudden, unexpected order to "move on" just when every one is settling down to the new berth, and to friendly acquaintance with the hosts. It is the last straw, they say; but in a wonderfully short time the battalion is swinging down the road with the usual song and jest, and the French mayor of the hamlet, with despairing shrugs but genial energy, is providing a new billeting officer, with a yet more English accent than the last, with a list of houses and barns capable of holding just so many officers and men.

It is a constant astonishment that all goes so smoothly between the French villager and the British soldier. They understand one another to a marvel, thanks to astounding feats of the sign language Numerals, a smile, a souvenir, and "no bonne" compose most of the vocabulary, but it suffices not only for necessities but as a foundation for friendly intercourse; and the incidents and requirements of the successive battalions are so similar that as the war lengthens a real *lingua franca* grows and develops.

The relationship is not easy or natural. War does not mellow manners among soldiers or civilians, and standards of morality turn many a cat-i'-pan on occasion. The British soldier may steal directly and the French civilian indirectly; but when all is said or thought, I have never ceased to wonder at the mutual friendship. "They are very kind," say the French villagers, especially those who have children, "and very generous"; and when things go at all wrong, "Que voulez-vous? Ce sont les soldats" - a shrug is all the complaint. We bring money into the villages, and it is appreciated, though devices for evading billeting duties are common. You may not by French law billet on a lone woman or in an inn. So some women banish the rest of the household till the house is taken off the billeting list, and others, with the aid of a good easy mayor, convert their home into an inactive inn, - or "estaminet" - called by our soldiers a "jestaminute." Nevertheless, amity reigns. On the whole, the men are popular, more popular perhaps than the officers, who do not arouse any sense of pity and whose approach is stiffer. Yet they too like their hosts and are liked. I heard the full tale of one marvellous Australian fight round

Pozières from a fighting colonel while he sat at tea at a most dapper little table and interrupted his story by sallies in the most amazing French with three hostesses, who hung on his lips and begged for interpretation of any detail they missed. And they missed many, for the colonel's French was little better than the ladies' English. Three Desdemonas drank the words of one Othello, and the scenic effort was enhanced by the real boom of cannon and a view of streets full of soldiers.

The billets may be anywhere and of any sort, under fire of guns or behind divisional headquarters. They may be tents or dugouts or Armstrong huts, or now and again, as often in July, in the open air. But more men are billeted in houses than elsewhere; and the companionship with French villagers is part and parcel of the normal life. In the villages nearer the line, the stay is often short, for the incomers may be on the move to a real rest behind. They may be carried on their way by 'buses and lorries; but for the most part they go on Shanks' mare, and cover long reaches.

Once in the high heat of summer I saw a few men fall out and lag while the worried officer rode to and fro in perpetual effort to keep the battalion together. But only once. The training and the spirit of the troops are equal to the demand whatever the season; and dog-tired and sleepless with days and nights of fighting, battalions still swing along with something of that athletic spring which stirred French villagers to a frenzy of admiration along the line of country whence we chased the flying Germans in the first September of the war. "Your athletics serve you well," said an old French doctor whom I then met. "Never did I see men before who so danced when they walked."

It is a moving Odyssey, the return from the trench, at whatever point you touch it: at the furtive slipping away in the dark or dusk, at the grouping and roll call, during the long plod across the field and along the alleged roads, where perhaps a general meets and greets and praises them, or towards its end, along the real roads of a safe land, when the men pull along the hand trollies almost with the dogged silence of animals; and the expectation of immediate sleep takes off the jauntiness of the enemy's helmet, substituted for the hat, and reduces the bubbling delight in the more solid trophies - the enemy's machine-guns pulled on the trollies among a medley of various kit.

It is a moving Odyssey; but the spectacle of the men marching forward carries a deeper appeal. The companies are all at full strength, and you are not tempted, as you see them pass, to tragic and vain counting of the toll of battle. The men walk more briskly and sing more readily; but the vivacity and expectancy of the hours before battle have a poignancy, peculiar and irresistible. On 1st July and at various attacks the attacking troops were marked with bright patches of colour, triangles of yellow or whatnot, fixed to their back. Ticketed and docketed, they went forward to the great adventure in a spirit and with a manner so matter of fact, so free from the flamboyancy of glory, the affectation of heroism, or the dullness of mere obedience that your admiration and wonder were left without handle or, as it were, excuse. Their simplicity left you no sentimental refuge from hopes and fears already too poignant to endure.

This simple modesty of manner never fails them. On the way up to see an attack at Thièpval, I met in a very narrow communication trench some of the Warwickshire troops coming back from a peculiarly brilliant fight. They had won important trenches and endured very heavy fire for three days. It was difficult to pass in the trench, which was greasy and narrow, with few bags; and it was impossible to leave it with any safety. As we struggled past one another and made way for one another, and now and then, when there was a block, talked with one another, I could detect no sign in any one of them of pride or weariness or elation. Knowing their record, one desired to do or say something appreciative or congratulatory, to express admiration or excitement; but the men were too wholly unself-conscious. They apologized for the difficulties of passing, and spoke of the weather as if the communication trench to a field of death and glory, strange and terrible beyond imagination, were the street way to daily work.

The manner of men who are coming out or going in differs as much as their behaviour on the field. Different countries differ; but there is a strong English likeness between all English troops. I make no invidious comparisons between soldiers from different parts of the Empire. They fight in different ways. Their virtues emerge in different forms. Their courage has different features - that is all. In possession of courage all are at the top. The peculiar form of English courage is chiefly shown, I think, in the power to "stick it."

An engagement had been won on the flank of these Warwickshires by Sussex troops through the virtue of mere quiet, dutiful obstinacy. Relief could not reach them easily, and they were needed to make an attack over ground they knew. So they waited, they "stuck it" for more than a week, not as an achievement in itself but as a preparation for an attack. Their long endurance just tuned them up for the aggressive venture that was meditated; and you must cultivate a vivid impression of what artillery fire is before you can understand what such patience means. No one will ever know what this backing of good old English county obstinacy has done for the success of our armies.

In the particular action which followed, heroic deeds, though many, less impressed themselves on the fighters' memories than what I may call the idiomatic ways and behaviour of the men. "Not so much of your 'mercy' and more of your 'come along'" said one soldier to a trembling captive, as if he thought "mercy" a rather silly, affected literary sort of word to use.

A sergeant, who had nothing but an empty Verey-light pistol, covered and cowed a German officer who held an automatic pistol fully loaded. The two men met face to face in a German trench and looked at one another "it seemed for a minute" before the German's pistol dropped and his hands went up, with the confession, made in perfect English, "Friend, I've had enough." The sergeant "stuck" the duel of looks the longer.

And when it was all over, never were soldiers less full of rancour or bitterness than these essentially English troops. They are as little intoxicated at victory as disturbed by suffering. All words of praise and high admiration, all big words about heroism and patriotism, all thoughts of dramatic ecstasy fall to the ground before such soldiers. They are just English; and the word will serve. It is not easy perhaps to find a better.

CHAPTER XIII
TANKS AND OTHER ENGINES

THE most stirring day in all the Somme battle was 15th September, when that ingenious engine, soon familiarized into the Tank, was introduced - came out. It is a pity the Tanks were not invented in the time of the Little Picts. They are made for tough little men, who can stow themselves away anywhere. For the Tank in reality, as opposed to the Tank in fiction, is a lowly and humble monster, leaving little room for the Jonahs who inhabit him, and seeking the obscurity of the latest *camouflage*.

Their inconspicuousness served them well. Seldom was a weighty secret better kept. The enemy had only a few days' warning of the arrival of a "British armoured car," and for once in a way the general public - and indeed the army - had no hint of their arrival in France. It was regarded as the highest privilege when some of us were allowed to investigate them, to enter their cribbed cabin and talk with the little -men, wearing their padded leather helmets, who inhabited them. Even five months after their appearance their finer points are still obscure to the multitude and, it is hoped, to the enemy.

They enjoyed, nevertheless, a dramatic debut. To see a rank of these jaundiced Batrachians awaiting under the slope of the hill their nocturnal advance to the firing line, gave one the sort of shiver belonging to the unknown. I confess to a personal terror, and nursed fears that they would turn and rend our own people or inspire fallacious hopes. The fears were vain, if not wholly vain. The terror they inspired was wholly the enemy's and the humour wholly ours.

They lay in hiding, after several nights on the road, some mile or so behind the line on the evening of 14th September, awaiting the great attack of the 15th. A gibbous moon and brilliant stars, shining in an almost frosty night, lit with fantastic shadows and crescent patches of light the earth-craters and parapet ridges of the bare highland; and as the night yielded to the dawn, the colours on the backs of the monsters shifted like a chameleon's. How soon would the enemy see them? The hands of the wrist watches were moving close to zero time. Soon after six the spasmodic barking of the night-time cannonade (normal in spite of its intensity) gave place to a "kettledrum bombardment." The "fun" was "fast and furious," and two minutes after the orchestra opened our men leaped from their trenches. The secret was still intact. In spite of the harvest moon, we had brought up a certain number of the "armoured cars" against which the Germans had been warned. "Autos blindôs" is the French term. They looked like blind creatures emerging from the primeval slime. To watch one crawling round a battered wood in the half-light was to think of "the Jabberwock with eyes of flame" who

"*Came whiffling through the tulgey wood
And burbled as it came.*"

Though now the sun was near the edge of our world - just at this hour I saw the strings of shrapnel clouds fired against our aircraft redden at its touch - though moonlight and sunlight struggled to give distinctness to the world, the enemy ill distinguished the guise of these iron monsters, which in truth amused our men rather than encouraged them. They were a jest, a cause of cheerfulness; possibly faithful creatures, but no rival to the bayonet.

One German officer said it was "an impertinence" to use them; and some of the German soldiers regarded them with a sort of superstitious terror for the first few minutes, till daylight disclosed their true nature.

Even then they were alarming enough. With ludicrous serenity they wobbled across the gridiron fields and shook themselves as if the bullets were flies that bit just deep enough to deserve a flick. Those who had inspected these saurians in their alfresco stalls beforehand or followed their lethargic course over impossible roads in the moonlight gasped with humorous wonder at the prodigy. Munchausen never approached the stories imagined for them by soldiers. But their pet name will always be "Tanks," and they were chiefly regarded as a practical joke. Whales, Boojums, Dread-noughts, slugs, snarks - never were creatures that so tempted the gift of nicknaming. They were said to live on trees and houses and jump like grasshoppers or kangaroos.

But little real reliance was placed in them. The Germans had brought into warfare many forbidden forces - foul gases and living fire and the rest. We were to answer them with a British novelty, but one well within the rules of international law, and demanding the highest courage in those who used it. The crews had the full pioneer spirit. The courage of the men who took this virgin journey in the Trojan motor-cars was rewarded.

We used about forty on 15th September, the day when the Tank "came out," and the forty had twoscore of different experiences. Some one in the ranks made a ballad on the lines of the two little nigger boys of the Tanks that progressively vanished; but the ballad could not finish, because a number still remained. At two parts of the line the failure was conspicuous, but everywhere else points were won by their help. Three broke down on the right between Bouleaux Wood and Ginchy, and three were arrested in High Wood; but even the wrecks met with adventures. The engine that had charge of the extreme right in Bouleaux Wood heeled over and lay on its side just inside the wood like a stranded whale. But it served for a body of Patroclus, a nucleus for the fight. British and German patrols shoved up close to its protecting bulk and there lobbed bombs at one another without decisive issue.

Much the same thing happened later in St. Pierre Divion, where for a while the Tank lay motionless in the midst of the enemy, who quite surrounded it. The Tank became a fort, beleaguered but invincible, spitting death all the time. Several were among the enemy's lines for a considerable time, and one was entered and probably photographed; but none was captured. The crew of one met a very heroic end. They came out of their machine, fought "on the floor" and at the end the commanding officer was seen calmly dressing wounds in the midst of a concentration of rifle fire.

The Tanks did not make the success of the day, but they did good service. One was able to pursue a number of Germans some way down the Bapaume road, and took prisoners. Some trenches were enfiladed by them, and useful firing was recorded of a Tank which entered Flers, where it walked down the ex-High Street amid cheers.

Several had dashing adventures. One appeared to "break into flames and smoke," but was in truth shaking off from its pachyderm the petty insults of German bombers. "We got nothing from them but blue sparks," said one captured machine gunner of the enemy.

The tale of individual experiences leaves imagination aghast; and yet the animals go about their daily business with so matter-of-fact an air in the midst of such a humorous bombing that you can scarcely think of them as anything but comic. In the evening a mile behind the battle one waddled round over the shell holes to call on a brigadier, just as a motor-car might stop at a front door. He was entitled "Cordon Rouge." His hide was dented all over by bullets, and his eyes had been several times put out. But the animal was entirely unmoved by a series of experiences at which imagination boggles. The driver had just come round on his way to the garage to say that "Barkis was willing" if and when wanted.

All this in the midst of intermittent shell explosions among scenes that outdo Dore's "Purgatory." One which reached within 500 yards of Combles was hit, and could only go forward or backward. So it went forward, preferring death or glory: "The little Revenge ran on." Again she was hit and stopped. The commander still stuck to his ship and lay in the trough fighting successions of bombers and other enemies. At last, after five hours of this, when nothing more was to be done, the crew slipped out of the little side door on the lee side and made good their retreat with one casualty. The hulk lies there for days unapproachable by either side, like a neighbour Tank, that served in its wretched state as a trench barrier, with Germans on one side and ourselves on the other.

The Tank did not desert its humour even in the midst of battle. It is said to be authentic that one of them nosed down the street of Flers amid cheers, evoked especially by a notice on its side, "Great Hun Victory." That is the sort of humour which no German can understand.

Possibly the humour has been overdone. The Tank is a real engine of war; and the highest, sternest courage was required of the men who boxed themselves up and, embarked on this new thing, sailed straight into the hottest parts of the fight.

It is probable that German kite balloons saw them approach the previous day. It is certain that wherever possible guns were turned upon them. Some were hit by shells and the men who manned them killed. The crews indeed needed, as the ancients said, "the triple brass of courage" all the more for being encased in metal. At Courcellette, where a German battalion commander came out and gravely surrendered to the monster; at Martinpuich, at Thièpval, at Flers, the Tanks, those humorous Juggernauts, won points and saved good British lives.

Men followed them cheering; and in one spot the deepest disappointment was caused when a leading Tank sheered round and appeared to lose heart. But she was like the "Warspite," who made circles in the Jutland battle. The steering gear was temporarily disarranged, or the shell holes unusually complicated; the rather fussy, earwig-like wriggle of the heavy thing was enhanced for the moment. That was all. Soon she was on the forward march again, shooting like a fury; and the cheers were renewed.

In this war few great successes have been won by any new engine or force after the element of surprise was gone. The Tank is at least a possible exception. Doubtless on 15th September their novelty added to their terrors and accentuated their successes; but the engine had many subsequent adventures in which it saved the life of friends and destroyed enemies.

In the great September attack we were checked for a night by the sunken roads running into Gueudecourt. The village fell the next morning before infantry advancing in the wake of a Tank.

The animal advanced on a lone venture. With the unerring scent of the wild beast it went straight for the prey. It nosed down the trench and side of the sunken road, spitting fire all the time, and either shrivelling up its prey or driving victims before it. After it had cleared out the worst nest it was still insatiable, and waddled on sniffing. At one place a number of enemy surrendered to it, tying handkerchiefs to guns in hope of catching the monster's attention.

The affair of this monster seemed so interesting that an eagle-eyed bird of prey swooped down to within 400 feet to join in the sport; and the rattle of the airman's Lewis was added to the Tank's machine-guns. But the aeroplane left the beast to its final triumph. Tired and hot and a little lame, it rested for a while from its labours. At once all its enemies in the neighbourhood, and they were legion, swarmed round it and attacked it as the Lilliputians attacked Gulliver. They threw their petty bombs at it, they swarmed on to its back and fired rifles absurdly at supposed chinks and cracks in its hide.

All the while spits of fire issued from the monster's side and front, and Germans lay dead and wounded like wolves before a stag at bay. Perhaps the little men would have won in the end. I do not know. But the beast's friends, our infantry, had now come up. The enemy fled; but many score lay dead and wounded round it. A little later in the morning Gueudecourt was ours.

Tanks and their crews played a useful, if not vital, part in the engagements which led six weeks later to the complete capture of that 40-acre plot of monastic vaults and rubble which is called Eaucourt l'Abbaye. It was defended by the trench system composing the old German third line, which we took everywhere except at a point south of Eaucourt. Here the wire was uncut, and our attacking troops lay down in the open in front of the wire, throwing and receiving bombs.

Mills bombs and egg bombs made rival festoons in the air over the wire. It was a duel in which the German was likely to get the better of the exchange, as he had a good trench and we had not. Happily, at this juncture intervened, as in the play, "the god from the machine." Some Tanks squirmed out from their lairs behind a copse on the left, and slugged forward almost in Indian file. They crossed the German trenches, and immediately nosed along them as if they had struck a scent trail, making mincemeat of all obstruction.

One of the machines "absolutely ate up the wire," as a soldier said, and, in spite of every kind of fire, continued its solemn course. The infantry crossed in its wake, some occupying the trench, some pushing through and past the buildings to a trench line which they fortified beyond on the north. The Tank could not go on for ever. Bogged and out of breath, it came to a stop in an impassable pit, with a half of the trench still uncleared.

The crew escaped and had strange experiences. One wounded officer took refuge in a shell hole well within reach of German bombers. Three of his companions refused to leave him, while a fourth went for help. After a strange journey he dragged himself to headquarters with his last ounce of bodily and mental strength, too exhausted even to give any clear account of the exact whereabouts of the shell hole. But his information was of value, and after some rest he himself set off again with others and rediscovered the true bearings.

Later again, though none was used in the first advance, a Tank was used with effect in the reduction of a redoubt in front of Beaumont-Hamel. The success was not altogether legitimate, perhaps, for it was won after the engine became motionless; and yet it is the highest compliment to say that it is most dangerous when at bay, and, like Mr. Kipling's Fuzzy Wuzzy, is "generally shamming when it's dead."

Some form of the Tank is probably a permanent engine of war. It was tried in conditions incomparably worse than any ever imagined. Its crews were necessarily amateurs, and infantry commanders exist who cannot speak with patience of it. They are mostly men who fought in the woods, where the combination of shell hole and tree was insuperable. Nevertheless, the Tank - lowly, heavy, obscure, slow, noisy, variable; - plods on, and will remain a high tribute to British mechanical skill.

We answered in mechanics to the enemy's chemical innovations. Doubtless the Germans are good chemists; but there is no novelty in any of the chemical devices used in this war. The chlorine gases were known to be deadly and heavy, and their use in war was new only because the world had decided that they were too inhuman. Higher ingenuity was shown in the gas shell, which completely ousted cylinder gas in the

Somme battle. Towards the end of July the Germans produced a quite new shell. It acted differently and contained a new gas. At one place they poured these shells over in thousands. Just over five thousand fell on an acre or two near the point of junction of the French and British armies one afternoon. These shells burst almost without noise. They were at first supposed to be "duds." The cap just rolled off, and a gas not strong in scent, nor obvious to the eyes, oozed out. Its effect was not instantaneous; the victim was indeed not aware that he was gassed till several hours afterwards, when he collapsed suddenly. But only a very full breath was deadly; and when men became aware of the nature of the shell, little harm was done.

Yet the gas shell has been used more and more. The enemy shot hundreds every night of the Somme battle, and the French became great experts in their use. Some of the most desperate attacks, such as the storming of Pozières, were delivered by masked men, volubly cursing the necessity of charging in a half -blind state. Every rood of the battle-field is littered with masks, German and British; and every trench and even remote billets are ornamented with gongs for giving the gas alarm. One of the best series of photographs taken in the course of the battle was spoiled because a sentry rushed into the dark room where they were being developed, with an alarm of gas, caused by a single shell.

The "tear" or lachrymatory gas shell is used by the enemy chiefly with the object of damping down a troublesome battery for the time being. It has had the desired effect on occasion; and the fumes will make the eyes tingle several hours after the shell has exploded. The paraphernalia of helmets has added to the cost and burden of fighting; and doubtless in any future wars, if such must be, gas shells will be employed for this reason alone. But whether they do as much harm as high explosives and shrapnel is by no means clear; though doubtless an attacking force compelled to use masks is by reason of the mask a much less efficient fighter.

The enemy is proud of having invented the "Flammenwerfer," or flame-thrower, though his instruments are less good than ours; and they have been used more and more, sometimes with effect. Our artillery destroyed several in High Wood, before the great attack. But the flame is not effective against men who have gone to ground, and its utmost limit of reach is about 100 yards. For this reason it should be more effective in defence than in attack. But the logic of these things disappears before the intensity of high-explosive shells. Engines of all sorts are destroyed or buried or put out of action; and many an engine is only useful when it can be wielded in comparative serenity and with due preparation.

Yet flame and heat as against explosive is a developing principle. We have flame shells which can scorch to ashes anything within their range, and the Germans use flame balls of many sorts and sizes to attack aeroplanes. During the course of the Somme battle the old incendiary shell was improved and developed beyond recognition.

The stimulus to invention has been one of the most obvious effects of the war. All engines of destruction have improved, notably the automatic rifle - now capable of holding clips of twenty and more cartridge - with its telescopic and periscopic sights. The aeroplane has become almost a safe chariot. Even miners have discovered new tools. Edison was said to have wept at the sight of the waste of power in the waves and tides of the sea. It needs no such scientific imagination and emotion as his to weep for the waste of energy in the war. Such mental, such muscular, such material output might have saved Europe from the curse of poverty and left blessings to accumulate at compound interest for the peoples yet to be. Instead it has pashed out good and useful and happy lives in millions, destroyed the wealth and beauty of tens of thousands of homes, and so devastated many fair acres that they will never again produce food in the time of this generation.

So thick is the whole field with unexploded bombs and shells that no ploughman's life will be safe for years. Already peasants who have attempted to light a wood fire near the site of their vanished homes have been blown to atoms.

Such is the fruit of material Kultur unsweetened by the breath of spiritual hope.

CHAPTER XIV
THROUGH PRISONERS' EYES

I N A PLEASANT chateau behind the front were housed during a great part of the Somme battle the staff of one of the corps most actively engaged. On the grass beside a flaming rose-bed stood a line of the absurdest instruments to which garden ever gave entertainment. They were the spoil of the right, a battery of the most primitive trench mortars conceivable. Mechanism they had none. They were no more than long tubes about 10 inches in width bound outside with coiled wire and lined inside, over the lowest third of their circle, with thin iron plates. They threw just lumps of explosive from a range of about 200 yards, and were useful enough for destroying earthworks and trenches. I measured one hole made by them just behind a Kemmel earthwork as 19 feet. These mortars were the only obvious signs of the neighbourhood of war, though we were close behind the line.

The interior of the chateau, on the other hand, was all war. In every room officers were busy with maps: one piecing together air-photographs; another drawing blue, red, and green lines - the sequent objectives of the next attack. Another was collating a mass of German letters and post cards and note -books. This last one asked if I would do something for him. Would I carry three baskets of carrier pigeons up to "the advanced cage"? The intelligence officer provided me with three basketfuls, which were piled on the car. Hurrying away with the burden, I was met some miles away by an officer, entirely unknown to me, who signalled violently and stopped his car and mine. Then he introduced himself as "Officer Commanding pigeons"; and "O.C. pigeons" is a proud position. Pigeons have been at least as successful as any other means of communication. They are trustworthy, quick, and authentic.

They have won many fights and saved many defeats. Quite a number of the birds from first to last have been killed by shrapnel - three fell almost together at the battle of Loos - but over all the field the percentage is minute; and you may rely on nine out of ten pigeons finding their way home.

The pigeon specialists are a group of importance, and have this point of pre-eminence that they give the letter postmen more trouble than all the rest of the army put together. But the army post office is a most determined agency, and though it costs a ton of motor-cycle oil, they hunt down these vagrant pigeon men till they find them, and reduce to the minimum the tale of undelivered letters.

One humorous and quite true tale of the pigeon has gone the rounds and appeared as fiction in "Punch" with some altered details. A colonial soldier carried one of the baskets all through an engagement, but was not called upon to "enlarge" his birds. Being a wise man he did not see the necessity of carrying the burden home, so he released the birds after attaching a short note to one. The belief is that at the headquarters the staff were thirsty for authentic news. So eager were they that when the pigeon appeared the general ordered it to be shot if it did not at once return to hand. When finally the bird delivered its message, excitement grew intense. The general unrolled the slip, and while others craned their necks to see, he spelled out with trouble this message: "I'm fed up with carrying this bird!"

The pigeons I carried were judged by the O.C. to be well-kept birds and carefully tended, so we took them on to the advanced cage. It swarmed with Prussians. They stood and sat and lay behind the walls of barbed wire, busy with a score of domestic occupations. Some had pulled off their shirts and were hunting industriously for the lice that infest the clothing of almost all soldiers who live for any length of time in the trenches. Some were scraping off mud with bits of apple-twig plucked from the trees among which they were caged. In one compartment the new-comers were devouring bully beef and biscuits wolfishly and with hurried gusto. Two officers stood dour and fierce in a wired room by themselves. A dozen or so had been taken from the cages and were sitting in a row undergoing in turn inspection from a doctor. Two were being interrogated by interpreters who looked more fagged than the prisoners, for the stream had been continuous and each group must be moved on quickly to make room for the rest that were momently expected. The prisoners never rest in the cages, but are moved back to more luxurious spots as quickly almost as our own wounded.

I have met prisoners coming back from the battle in every guise and temper, and their groups remain in the mind as the vividest evidence of battle, the most palpable symbol of defeat. On the slope below Thièpval I saw them leap from their trenches with hands up and, before there was full time to accept the surrender, run in panic down the hill to our lines through the random German shells. One group, hustling across the valley below me, was quite blotted out by a shell, and a single man afterwards killed by a naval shell nearly ten miles behind the lines. As a rule they recover cheerfulness as soon as they swallow the first drop of water, and again and again express their utter pleasure to be safe out of the battle. The cheerfullest of all the prisoners' faces that come back to me was a fair, round, smiling countenance of a corporal who belonged to a pioneer battalion, captured in Flanders. He was one of the last to scramble into a lorry that was taking them out of shell range, and his feelings overcame him. He put his head round the canvas at the back of the van, waved a sandbag which he had converted into a hat and shouted, "Off to the best city in the world - London," and his intonation was almost Cockney.

This man's sergeant was cheerful from a different reason. He argued with charming logic that the war would soon be over. "You see" he said, "we shall take Verdun, though it cost us 300,000 men, and then the French will be broken and you will have to give in or take a beating, whichever you like."

Among soldier prisoners rancour or resentment is as rare as it is common among officers; and our own men, even the conductors, seldom keep up any pretension of hate. More commonly they treat the prisoner as they would a favourite dog. After one very bitter engagement I met two wounded men hobbling back, one a Cockney, the other a

Bavarian. "Wherever I goes Fritz goes, don't you, Bill?" he said; and now and again he gave Bill Fritz two or three puffs of his cigarette, holding it carefully while the German pulled. This utter failure of resentment in face of the sight of a single human being is common to most of us; perhaps.

In the first month of the war I walked to a Paris hospital with a famous civilian who breathed a doctrine of blood and thunder against the brutes who had disturbed the world's peace. He spoke forcibly an excellent doctrine, and went even to the length of preaching hard treatment of prisoners. In the first ward we visited happened to be one wounded German, and my companion spoke as kindly to him as to the rest. He spent, I think, a little longer at his bedside; and I know he presented him, and him only, with a large and costly cigar. As a race we are not good at hating men and women, and in this part of war at any rate must frankly acknowledge German superiority.

Even on the battle-field itself, or just behind it, many soldier prisoners achieve a certain look of satisfaction. They are alive - against all probabilities; and they are thankful. Nevertheless, no episode in war can on occasion touch a higher note of tragedy. On the 3rd of July, as I was pushing up the road through Fricourt village, a north-country soldier was bringing down a mad German soldier of the 111th Regiment whom he had captured in a redoubt at the corner of the wood, and the sight is not uncommon. In every battle there are men, both from victors and vanquished, who go mad, with one form or another of the malady. One of our N.C.O.'s, who had fought gloriously at Loos, and had returned to safety, suddenly seized a rifle, fixed the bayonet, attempted to stab a neighbour, and then ran as fast as he could travel straight for the German trenches.

That day in Fricourt I saw something worse than madness, unless it was, after all, madness. A German Hauptman, stiff, erect, obstinate, but with a strange look in his eyes, marched down the road in front of his captor. As I moved a step nearer to read the number on the shoulder strap, the German started with a sudden nervousness curiously contradictory to his general bearing. He was bareheaded, but otherwise more neat and clean than the prisoner often is. Afterwards, I learned that the hatlessness betrayed the tragedy behind his obvious terror. He had surrendered, but had first hidden a bomb in his cap, and as two British officers came up to interrogate him he threw the bomb between them. No wonder he was afraid. It was amazing that he had lived so long.

How very different were the bearing and actions of the German captives met in a similar place on a similar day a fortnight later. At 3.30 in the morning of 14th July we sprang at the German second line and took it by storm. We captured Bazentin le Petit, Bazentin le Grand, Longueval, a part of Delville Wood, and the land between them. In tactics no victory surpassed it, and the rush was so quick that numbers of prisoners began to filter back within an hour or two. For the first time in the war they were turned to real use, and a squad of forty or fifty volunteers offered to bear back wounded, German or British, as might be. They carried the majority across the little valley and up the winding road to Mametz village. Such a scene as this strange tryst I had never seen. Three roads meet near the crown of the hill, and in the wide space at their meeting-point a great crowd was gathering. The hill-road was hastily botched by hurried menders. They poured brick rubble into the shell holes, filled up the trench at the side, tossing into it bits of dead horses and the refuse of the battle. Through them swayed and grunted the Red Cross lorries whose terminus was this Trivia in the village.

Desolation at its highest power encircled the place. Roadmen were hacking down any bit of brick wall that was left. Blackened beams, tiles, weapons, and intolerable flotsam of rubbish covered the site of every village home; and in the very centre of the whirlpool assembled and multiplied our wounded soldiers. They sat and lay and stood - chaffing, talking, groaning, silent. Blood soaked their clothes and disguised their faces and mixed with the mud on their thighs. But most were "walking cases." Sometimes the walk was a crawl or a hop, helped by a pair of friends almost as halt as the man they helped. It was my duty to walk farther, and see the country beyond, where the righting was. I had gone not 200 yards farther round the left-hand road and over the shoulder of the hill when I met a line of Bavarians, looking like a funeral procession. They tramped slowly into view in groups of six, each six carrying a stretcher. They were mingled anyhow with our own wounded, with messengers going forward and messengers coming back; but they had the appearance of some solid thing among fugitive things: a barge plodding down a river, or a hearse in a busy street. They did their business very well - slowly, methodically, carefully, silently. "It is better than fighting," they said and felt. They were leaving danger behind. They were under orders. They were promised beef and biscuit and drink.

Suddenly every man ceased to be a soldier. The counterfeit presentment broke up like the model of the clown in the old transformation scene. Militarism fell from them the moment they walked in uneven order. The house of cards collapsed. A battalion became a group of individuals: the peasants were peasants again, the professors professors. Some thought of beef, some of philosophy. "I prefer your bully," said one rough fellow; but the schoolmaster began a disquisition. "The directors of Germany have invested our money in a venture which has somewhat of the appearance of a gamble; but it is impossible to get our money out, and we must support the directorship so long as there is a chance of saving the capital. If that is lost, we shall institute an inquiry, and depose the directors, perhaps imprison them."

The doctor only spoke of the madness of the world and the sanctity of the human body. A natural philosopher said, with the first touch of humour, that he was "going to try to like the English."

All this was after they had traipsed off the field and collected in groups in a square of barbed wire. They might have been monkeys; but they were at least on the way to become men.

Very early in the war cool observers described the prisoners as inferior, as depressed, as showing signs of demoralization - and the verdict was seldom justified. The truth is, it is very hard to judge a large group of men. As a rule they are covered with mud and have just come through trials severe and various enough to destroy sensation. Sometimes they have been quite cut off from food and drink for many hours. Men, even tough soldiers, do not look their best at such times.

An observer in the position of a war correspondent, who travels daily across a stretch of ten or fifteen miles before reaching the front, sees prisoners almost every day. I have seen thousands in all parts of the field since the Somme opened, and many score in the previous six months. Their quality progressively depreciates. Of that there can be no question. The worst in physique were the men taken at and round Beaumont-Hamel on 13th November.

Our men actually pitied them for their deep dugouts, and seemed to regret that these did not permit the poor fellows to get out in time to fight with the bayonet. You could almost infer the same fact from the mere spectacle of the prisoners. I met a thousand or so of them on their way back to the "cages" shepherded by little groups of King Edward's Horse, and could see in them small sign of battle. They were comparatively clean, and looked curiously white, as if they had seen little sunshine or even daylight. It is,, indeed, literally true that dugout existence, coupled with the fear of movement by day, has bleached a great part of the German army.

But many of these troops were not of the most lusty sort. They were largely Silesians, old soldiers, but composing one of the newer divisions pieced together out of the superfluity of old divisions. The shoulder straps on the groups that passed me denoted the 55th, 62nd, 2nd, 68th, and 23rd Regiments.

Though not perhaps the keenest soldiers, they had some excuse for their too easy surrender. In parts of the line the enemy were certainly taken by surprise - by the sudden completeness of the barrage and the dash of our troops - and little fight was left in them. Our men went rather quicker than usual, in spite of the mud. Some waves hurried straight over the first three trenches, which they found pulped into shapelessness by our fire, and even before they reached the fourth a long string of Germans came filing out towards them with hands in air. Certain groups among them exhibited a humorous docility and humane readiness to assist their captors. For example, a Red Cross corporal, armed only with a stick, at once, unasked, drilled a group of nine of his infantry into stretcher-bearers and set them to work in the middle of the fight. They did their journey without loss, for happily the enemy's shelling was not severe; and the machine-guns at this place were mostly silent.

A few days earlier a large group were taken on the southern side of the Ancre, from a trench on the highland known as Regina. In spite of an order against the use of slang in official messages, the exact wording of the first message that reached Divisional Headquarters was: "Prisoners much fed up." It did not mean that they had over-eaten. The description was true, beyond all question. I met many of them on their way to be interrogated. They were of all sorts: Prussian Guards and Saxons. The first - a Red Cross man with a broken arm made a fine figure. The next was as pitiable a creature as you could find: about 5ft. 2in. in height, very unlovely in feature, shuffling in gait, and wearing immensely strong spectacles. Face and clothes were smeared all over with chalky mud. The third was a pleasant-looking Saxon, wounded above the ankle by a bomb.

Some of the prisoners (whom I only half believed as men too severely shaken to be accurate) wailed astounding stories of the ruin wrought by our artillery. Twenty-four companies, they said, had been totally wrecked. The exaggeration - if it was an exaggeration - was permissible; for our own men engaged in the attack agreed with observers behind it that it was the "prettiest" barrage they had worked with, intense, accurate, dashing, an excellent barrage to give a lead over the fence. One of this group, using the childlike idiom common among people much shaken by fear, said, "When I threw up my hands and called out, 'Good, kind enemy, mercy, mercy!' your men stopped throwing bombs, and one patted me on the shoulder and told me to go home to your lines." In the previous action in the same area a Canadian soldier told me that he had seen only one German really fight - a man already lying seriously wounded, who, pretending incompetence, threw a bomb at the head of the officer who came up to succour him.

It was not to be inferred from such examples that the enemy was fighting badly. The only part of the fighting at which he does not, as a rule, excel is the hand-to-hand; and when he curls up he curls up completely. It was so in this engagement. Fifty un-wounded prisoners who came back in one group were quite frankly delighted at their fate.

Perhaps the sight of prisoners, especially the soldiers' experience of cowering men creeping from dugouts, gives an exaggerated sense of the captors' superiority. No creature is more abject than a frightened captive. One man in Guillemont appeared on his knees at the mouth of a dugout, holding out in his arms all that he could collect of any value - watches, soda-water, bread, bayonets, cigars, bits of kit - begging the men who came up to spare his life. In another case the inmate of a dugout was so nervous that he did not know how to surrender. He kept waggling his hands outside the dugout, muttering "Kamerad," and then retiring precipitately like a hermit crab. By the time an assurance of safety was conveyed to his intelligence he had become quite exhausted by his gymnastics. The division which showed the greatest demoralization on this occasion had just come down from Armentières, where dugouts had been deep and life easy. The change to the Somme was too hard for them.

Such state of terror sometimes continues for a long while. Prisoners taken behind Ginchy came back weeping bitterly and thoroughly cowed; but both the tears and the depression were produced objectively, not, as I first thought, by a craven spirit. The scarred woods, desolate villages, and honeycombed fields reeked of gas fumes, through which the queues and groups of prisoners traipsed, wiping their eyes. In a desperate attempt to arrest the fire of our guns and temporarily to check the march of the supports, tear shells had been plentifully rained over the country-side. Some of these prisoners had tasted both varieties of gas - ours and their own - within an hour or so, and could do nothing else than weep.

One man I spoke with - a Bavarian, whose unit had fought well - had been driven by gas and explosives out of his trenches into the hospitality of No Man's Land and its genial shell holes. There he was cut off by a patrol and presently marched back through the sugary fumes of German weeping gas. He tasted indeed the full savour of war between the hours of four and six that day; and yet knew little of the sort of battle in which he had fought, for he was captured early at the very fringe of the battle front.

Almost always the men who have once surrendered are amenable and docile; though mutinies have been known. One large group in Courcellette, discovering that they outnumbered their captors, made one tentative effort to escape, and in Thièpval a group of sixteen prisoners, several of whom had concealed bombs, turned on their two conductors and wounded them. Happily the conductors were saved from death by a support that was coming up, and the survivors of the sixteen prisoners were rounded up.

When they reach the cages the men speak readily and evince no sulkiness, in abrupt contrast with their officers. If turned to work, they work well. Never did I see quicker and more thorough and, it appeared, more congenial work than the manufacture of a prisoners' camp by prisoners. Every man seemed a technical specialist - a builder, a decorator, a plumber, a landscape gardener - and the group converted a bare patch of stubble into a most habitable camp, with good buildings and neat pathways, within the space of two days.

Nothing in the fighting so advertised to British eyes the secret of German success as the organized completeness of this domestic work. What madness turned such constructive workers, who had the world at their feet, to destructive warriors!

We had taken between 1st July and 16th November over 30,000 prisoners, among them many picked troops. The biggest haul was on the last days; and for me the most impressive sense of victory was the sight after the capture of Thièpval of a group of 500 or 600 Prussians who were marched by Midland soldiers into the army corps cages. Big, fine men, well skilled in war, nursed in the traditions of a famous regiment, "ribbed and palèd in" among fortifications of a two years' growth, these companies of the 29th Prussian Regiment deemed themselves impregnable.

I see them there marching captives from the mud of battle as a symbol of Prussian militarism and its coming fall. Were they not captured, and more than as many like them killed, by Territorial "amateurs" and new artillery - and almost with impunity, though they fought hard? Their soldierly qualities and stubborn righting spirit were to me a stronger proof of the turn of the tide than the nice, quiet, comfortable handful of ten Saxons who surrendered without prompting a day earlier and were quoted everywhere as a proof of the demoralized spirit of the men. Victory is a positive, not a negative, achievement.

A distinction exists between the prisoner and the deserter, though on occasion such was the confusion of the righting it was not always easy to tell which was which. In the neighbourhood of Warlencourt one group of Germans (who may be called deserters or prisoners, as you please) took the risk of coming over to our trenches with their hands up. They were immediately threatened by one of their own machine-guns, lifted on to the parapet with intent to wipe them out. Happily the position was seized by our observers, who immediately opened a machine-gun barrage *to protect the Germans*, and keep down the heads of their own cannibalistic snipers and machine-gunners. Under this kindly curtain let fall by their enemies the Germans made their way to the refuge of British trenches.

One most human incident issued from this proceeding. In the trench to which these prisoners were hurried was a dugout used for a dressing station, and in it was lying a wounded German, with difficulty rescued by our stretcher-bearers the day before. By one of the strange coincidences of war, he proved to be the brother of one of the prisoners. The new-comer was quite overcome by the meeting. He embraced his brother again and again, stroked his hair, and, almost sobbing, repeated again and again, "We thought you were dead."

The meeting added the last touch to the delight of the prisoners in escaping from the war. Never was a group happier. As some of them swung their hilarious way through Mametz Wood homeward - if one may use the word - they laughed and hummed songs like a party of trippers. One man was anxious to know whether he might be allowed to visit "his friends in Newcastle." "It is a lovely city," he said.

Three times at any rate during the Somme fighting Germans were met strolling behind our lines; and the question was never settled whether they had missed their way, escaped from a prisoners' batch, or deserted. In one case five men were accompanied by a dog.

Deserters have at no time been numerous, as numbers go in this war, but groups of twenty have come over; and after the Somme battle was over, the trickle was quite constant. Like all deserters, the men talked to distraction. One may say that prisoners always tell less than the truth and deserters always more. Especially do they enlarge on their own hardships.

Throughout the battle of the Somme I saw almost daily letters written by Germans, both soldiers and civilians. Many official documents were captured. Prisoners and deserters talked freely. By these means and others we had continual glimpses of the German state of mind during the whole of the period.

The German, though he has sloughed off much of the sentimentality for which he was once famous, is still a being who delights to enlarge on his personal feelings, to pour forth his soul in letters. The High Command, realizing that the habit was dangerous, proposed to prevent letter writing of any effusive nature; but they found that the valve was necessary to the soldier. Without such emotional outlet he lost heart and what is called moral. He was less happy, less courageous. So the postal system was increased and improved. Twice we took trenches immediately after the arrival of the parcel post, and our soldiers much enjoyed the food of which most parcels consisted.

At every prisoners' cage stacks of letters and post cards were collated, though everything else was given back to the men. Nothing in their treatment pleased them more. I heard men pouring out voluble thanks for permission to keep photographs of the fair faces carried in their inner pockets.

The letters undoubtedly showed a progressive decline in the spirit of the men. Some prisoners taken as early as 1st July complained bitterly of their plight and the difficulty of getting food and water through perpetual curtain fire; but within the German ranks at that time was a strong feeling that they were winning by mere resistance the final battle of the war. This confidence did not survive the attack of 14th July, when the second line fell, by Bazentin.

After this period scores of letters complained in grim and sarcastic terms of the inferiority of German airmen. They wear iron crosses, they sit in the front stalls of the theatre at Lille, they claim the affections of all the beautiful ladies; but when Mr. Englishman comes along, they are off like a streak. Such was the burden of many a soldier's diary. At the same time, their fear of British airmen was almost superstitious. They described the crouching dread of every man and motor while daylight lasted. One man wrote to say that soon the Englishmen would swoop down and pull them out of their holes by the scruff of the neck.

As the time went on, the continual shelling more and more affected men's nerves. They were bombed in trains fifty miles behind the line. They were shelled in billets, they were shelled in support and relief and all along the lines of march, so that some units reached the front trench shorn of half their strength. They had great regard for their own artillery, as anyone must who has seen it at work; but there were certain "regrettable instances." Something very near a mutiny was caused by the immense losses in two battalions shelled by mistake. So bitter was the feeling that the High Command sent round a printed apology with a promise that "it should not occur again."

As the battle proceeded, the belief that Germany could win, clean vanished. The optimists thought that Germany could hold what she had won, and could so force an honourable peace; but the spirit of attack died out. Very fine counter-attacks were delivered at places, and not without success in some of the woods; but in the open none was carried through till picked battalions of the Guards were put in opposite Warlencourt at the end of October. The generals strove by speech and written orders to restore the offensive spirit. A German general's order of the day, taken in a November battle, urged the troops to stand firm by the promise of revenge. "We will see to it that we exterminate the British and French armies by such a hell as they have themselves created." But his promise also confesses his plight, acknowledges the hell.

It was not only the bursting shell and fear of attack that the enemy had to endure. The sights of the battle-field weaken men's fibre even more than the sounds. At an earlier date in the battle a German soldier wrote as follows:

"Trenches quite fallen in… Dead and buried were to be seen in masses in and out of the trenches… Six or eight men were lying near piled one on the top of the other. On the way to our 6th Company, which we found after a search of two and a half hours, there were just as many corpses and men buried by shells and men who had not been properly buried. We saw terrible sights."

The worst passages are omitted, but this is enough to hint what the enemy's soldiers endured, and the battle-field reveals acres of such spectacles. A number of men have not been able to endure it. Almost all - men, not officers - are glad to be prisoners. But the alleged German demoralization is physical, and the body recovers. When we relaxed, the enemy recovered quickly.

In the advance along the Ancre considerable groups were quite dazed. In one trench in a sunken road between three hundred and four hundred men gave themselves up to sixteen men, who were accompanied by a padre. Almost immediately that he saw the smallness of the party the chief officer shouted an order to recover weapons and attack. But when he was shot by one of the soldiers the "mutiny" was immediately quelled, and the rest marched away as obediently as if they were under their own officers.

No man can endure a continuance of heavy fire. One rather attractive German of good physique and lively spirit, taken in November, apologized to his captors for his easy surrender. "What were we to do?" he said in effect. "The barrage came down like a storm in the mountains. You could not see or hear, and then while we were blind and deaf the English bombs began to burst in the ravine through the mud and dust and smoke."

I tried by observation and inquiry at every part of the line to test without prejudice the question whether or not the German garrisons, at such places as Beaumont-Hamel, surrendered with the readiness of a demoralized force. Many of our own men came from the battle persuaded that the enemy was done for, but when all was known it was clear that the victory was due wholly to the violence of the attack: not at all to the lack of spirit in the enemy. Instances there are, of course, of despair and cowardice. Out of twenty prisoners amassed by one unit ten were mere deserters - and they came from a regiment of high reputation. They had been hardly tried, and a third bout of the battle of the Somme was more than their spirit could endure. If men are not relieved often enough and for a long enough time the best regiments become the worst supposing that artillery fire is constant. And the Germans are but men.

Only once did the German officers evince disgust with their own organization. Soon after the capture of Contalmaison fresh troops were thrown into the tangled open country north-west of the village, without proper instructions and without maps. What they said of their superior staff would not have disgraced a regimental dugout in British trenches at the second battle of Ypres.

The German officer keeps a stiff upper lip. But we had progressive evidence in plenty that he was appreciating more and more keenly the courage and skill of his opponents. He knew before July was out that he had grossly underrated our military quality. The most precise evidence was supplied by a general of fame.

General Sixt von Armin, commanding the 4th German Corps, wrote in the early weeks of August a report of about 15,000 words in length on the battle of the Somme and the lessons to be drawn from it. He covers the whole field of criticism, discussing methods of attack, of defence, of commissariat, of discipline, on the German side and incidentally on ours.

It is a thorough, sober military document, but packed with small, interesting details outside the field of tactics, throwing much light on the haphazard confessions of many prisoners. A discussion of the quality of our army was given pride of place. The first paragraph of all dealt with our infantry. The document was called:

Experiences of the IV. German Corps in the Battle of the Somme during July 1916

Under the heading "English tactics," Von Armin wrote:
"The English infantry has undoubtedly learnt much since the autumn offensive. It shows great dash in the attack, a factor to which immense

confidence in its overwhelming artillery probably greatly contributes. The Englishman has also his physique and training in his favour. Commanders, however, in difficult situations showed that they were not yet equal to their tasks. The men lost their heads, and surrendered if they thought they were cut off.

"It was most striking how the enemy assembled and brought up large bodies of troops in close order into our zone of fire. The losses caused by our artillery fire were consequently large. One must, however, acknowledge the skill with which the English rapidly consolidated captured positions.

"The English infantry showed great tenacity in defence. This was especially noticeable in the case of small parties, which, when once established with machine-guns in the corner of a wood or a group of houses, were very difficult to drive out."

After dismissing the infantry, he deals with the artillery:

"Particularly noticeable was the high percentage of medium and heavy guns with the artillery, which, apart from this, was numerically far superior to ours. The ammunition has apparently improved considerably.

"All our tactically important positions were methodically bombarded by the English artillery, as well as all known infantry and battery positions. Extremely heavy fire was continuously directed on the villages situated immediately behind the firing line, as well as on all natural cover afforded by the ground. Registration and fire control were assisted by well-organized aerial observation. All night the villages were also frequently bombarded by aeroplanes."

To the air he pays his highest compliment:

"The numerical superiority of the enemy's airmen, and the fact that their machines were better, were made disagreeably apparent to us, particularly in their direction of the enemy's artillery fire and bomb dropping.

"The number of our battle-planes was also too small. The enemy's airmen were often able to fire successfully on our troops with machine-guns by descending to a height of a few hundred yards. The German anti-aircraft gun sections could not continue firing at that height without exposing their own troops to serious danger from fragments of shell. This has produced a desire for the antiaircraft defences to be supplemented by machine guns; these must, if necessary, be supplied from the reserve stocks. A further lesson to be learnt from this surprisingly bold procedure on the part of the English airmen is that the infantry make too little use of their rifles as a means of driving off aircraft."

Only at the end of this long screed does he come to the question that most interests all soldiers, the question of food. He writes as ingenuously as any of his men might speak:

"All troops were unanimous in their request for increased supplies of bread, rusks, sausage, tinned sausages, tinned fat, bacon, tinned and smoked meat, and tobacco in addition. There was also urgent need for solidified alcohol for the preparation of hot meals. In various quarters the necessity for a plentiful supply of liquid refreshments of all kinds - such as coffee, tea, cocoa, and mineral waters - is emphasized still more. On the other hand, the supply of salt herrings, which increase the thirst, was found to be, as a general rule, very undesirable. There is no necessity for an issue of alcoholic drink in warm and dry weather.

"Similar requests for improved rations, suited to the prevailing conditions, when in position, were made by the artillery."

Von Armin was himself relieved before the end of the Somme, but we saw the fulfilment of several of his recommendations; and never was the food better than in the trenches taken on 13th and 14th November. Germany always gives her soldiers the best. Civilians may starve if they please; but the more food, the better soldier, is a recognized military maxim.

How different was Von Armin's mood from that of a wireless message sent to New York during July! It ran thus:

"The great allied offence is the most sanguine during the whole war, and is generally considered ended with awful loss of men mainly in the English ranks and only inconsiderable gain - three kilometres of front line held by one German division which retired to second trench 800 metres back. German military experts are jubilant because a minimal gain has resulted. The gigantic efforts of the Allies really constitute incontestable proof of the invincibility of Germany. German war correspondents, who thus far have kept rather silent on developments on the Western front during the last few days, this morning publish a lot of details and harrowing incidents of the most terrible man-to-man battling that ever took place in this or any other war. Osborn Invoss tells of mighty English gas attacks. The Germans just managed to adjust their gas masks, when the English were discovered creeping in dense mass through swaying mist on to German lines. Quickly the German artillery was notified, which directed a terrific curtain-fire behind on the creeping English lines. The Germans jumped out of their trenches, hiding behind parapets just in time. The enemy, to his great astonishment, finding the trenches empty, jumped into them. Germans arose from behind parapets and rained bombs upon the utterly surprised enemy below. The English too had bombs and flung them from below on the Germans. The slaughter was awful. Soon the stock of these missiles was exhausted on both sides. Germans jumped into trenches. Spent English managed to crawl out. Terrific carnage and struggle with rifle and bayonet among men who could not even see each other's faces as both parties were still wearing the gas masks which made them look more like grotesquely disguised merrymakers than warriors bent upon killing each other. And still dense waves of gas came sweeping on, which must have confounded the English artillery, for they rained shells upon their own men.

"There was no way against this cold' unmerciful German rifle fire; and machine-guns popping up in places where they thought life had been utterly extinguished by preceding English cannonade had panicky effect upon the few men not mowed down by them. Either their reserves would arrive too late or not at all. Their young inexperienced officers lacked decision often, and did not know how to act, which uncertainty was communicated to the men. When reaching enemy's wire entanglements, they often found them fully intact and trenches full of troops ready with the rifle and machine-guns where they promised to walk over. Fearful losses under these circumstances were so obtrusively obvious that most prisoners mention fantastic figure losses. One captain said English losses during the first two days' offensive, according to generally accepted estimate among officers, amounted from 80,000 to

100,000. All agreed their own artillery responsible for many of their casualties. These terrific losses have considerably stunned them. Those otherwise keen young fellows became disheartened by the surprising experience of the last few days. While the captives deplore the war, they are nevertheless convinced that England cannot lose. An elderly officer of large experience, and widely travelled, was convinced that the war would end in a draw. Subalterns were still wrapped in English arrogance; and while admitting the failure of the offensive, clung to the effect of the blockade which is bound to bring Germany to her knees sooner or later. All express the highest admiration for the German General Staff, which seemed to know more about English movements than their own generals."

The offensive continued four full months after this was written, and the Germans lost to us and the French 80,000 prisoners and suffered at least 200,000 casualties.

CHAPTER XV
THE FINAL FIELD

I N THE LATER part of the battle of the Somme, after we took Le Sars, some way down the slope whose crown we had set out to win, progress was stayed except along the highland south of the Ancre, where the 5th Army, who had been attacking more as the 4th Army attacked less, had taken the Schwaben and Stuff Redoubts and Regina Trench by almost daily attacks.

The rain fell day after day, drowning all opportunity for greater operations; and we knew that one greater operation was planned. Day after day the date was postponed. At headquarters weather charts for fifty years back had been studied; and October was found to carry a bad record. In 1916 she surpassed her old ill-records; and soldiers began to pray for November as if a change in name would involve a change in nature. Soon the change came. The days were too short and dark for a reform of the terrain. A dirty and sticky battlefield was certain; but if the ground became at all passable, the new attack was to be attempted. The 1st of July was recalled in many respects, though the contrast in appearance was altogether abrupt. The horizon shrank. The trees were bare. The ladder was taken down from a favourite observation tree. Shells penetrated deeply before exploding. Though the air was usually populous with aircraft, they could often see little. Yet the general change was not great. As you walked to the old observation point to see Beaumont-Hamel the shrapnel pattered down over the same stretch of road, and the high explosive whined on its way towards an alleged battery on the right. Once again, as on 1st July and again on 3rd September, we were about to make a frontal attack on the old German front line; and once again, day and night, our guns drummed. Each hour of each day the noise battered the ear. The sound was as constant as the touch of the atmosphere. Near the front it killed all sleep; and ten, even twenty, miles behind men woke to wonder what giant event the tumult portended. Groups of citizens in towns and women labourers in the village, farther off yet from the line, went to their doors to watch the winks of light, as of summer lightning, among the dusky clouds; and the shimmer was too constant to allow them to count the flashes.

As the second week of November came near its end, we noticed flecks of dust along the high road to Albert. "Has it come too late?" - The question was asked in all headquarters; and the answer was that it was late, but not too late.

On the morning of 1st July a soft and delicate mist, bediamonded by the sun, half concealed and half revealed the pillars of smoke and bodies of moving men. On the morning of 13th November a heavy, clammy fog blotted out your very neighbour, and dawn itself, which followed the opening of battle at near an hour's interval, was a secret performance. Soldiers lost touch with their neighbours before they had travelled a hundred yards, and stumbled over posts, scraggy with broken wire, into the very arms of shivering Germans.

How much we lost and how much we gained by the gloom no one may tell. It added to the surprise, it diminished initial casualties, but it hindered every detail in the organization of attack; and doubtless tactical blunders were committed by small units of the Naval Division unused to such land conditions. But the sum was good. The 1st of July was avenged, and never before had prisoners flowed into our cages in such mass and with so woebegone an air of utter defeat. From Beaumont-Hamel to the Ancre one wave after the other swept across these boasted defences and flooded the two villages of Beaumont-Hamel and of Beaucourt.

A terrible and vain battle with the mud was engaged north of this by a famous division, and north again Shropshire troops won trenches by skill and daring; but the battle, which coped the battle of the Somme, and won a further stretch of the two-year-old fortress, was chiefly in the charge of two divisions, one a naval division, fighting its virgin battle, the other a Scottish division.

The naval men moved along the Ancre, with their right resting on the river, their left on an imaginary line - often disregarded - separating them from the Scots. In the foggy gloom of 6 A.M. on 13th November the first waves went over, each carefully instructed to seize and occupy such and such a trench, and let succeeding waves go through them to such another objective; but it was not a day, and the men were not the men for precise and mathematical manoeuvres. Like some of the heroes whose names they fought under, the Drakes, Hawkes, and the rest won more by their spirit than by their learning. "They made tactical mistakes," said a general, "but did all, and more than, they had to do."

In a battle where every man fought nobly for the honour of his regiment and his country one individual act of leadership stands out in peculiar distinctness. Colonel Freiberg, already known for an adventurous career of his own choosing, and famous for a single-handed adventure in Gallipoli, was in command of the unit that advanced along the north bank of the River Ancre. He was wounded in the first rush over the parapet, but he had no intention of missing the great adventure for the handicap of a mere wound. He had seen many sorts of battles in different places. At one time he had found excitement in gun-running exploits in Mexico. He had won medals and distinction in Gallipoli; but a greater opportunity was now to his hand; he had the Nelson chance of putting the telescope to his blind eye.

The troops on his left were held up, but between him and them ran, roughly parallel with the line of advance, a friendly spur that cut off the spray of any raking machine-guns. Under its lee and along the south-easterly slope the attack prospered. Hundred yards was added to hundred yards; trench after trench passed and cleared. At one place the advance was a sort of leap-frog. As one line took a trench a fresh wave jumped their ditch and made forward to the next stopping-place. It was as if Jellicoe popped his hand on St. Vincent's shoulder.

But formal plans seldom survive unbroken the shock of battle. Elsewhere the impulse to chase the enemy or to get to grips - to board him - was overwhelming, and any medley of Drakes or Hawkes or who not raced forward together in common rivalry.

After fourteen hours' fighting - from the gloom of 6 A.M. to the darkness of 8 P.M. - this naval flotilla had crossed a mile of the roughest sea any sailor ever knew, and occupied a line of trenches and shell holes well within striking distance of Beaucourt village. Nor was this all. Three machine-guns were pushed forward well beyond this line, and, still insatiate, the wounded doctor-colonel-gunrunner-sailor-soldier asked leave to go on and attack the village. His men were at least 1000 yards in front of the companies on the left, endeavouring to advance across the north-westerly slope, and the position was essentially improper, as the edge of victory usually is. Everything suggested defence, not defiance. Numbers were not great. The men had fought like tigers without rest, and the majority were either out of action or in occupation of posts and trenches, or had gone back to hand over prisoners to little squads of cavalry.

But "the little Revenge" meant to run on. The better part of an assaulting battalion, say 500 men, was made up, swept together, and set in order. It amounted, perhaps, to three companies, with another in support. The night was well spent in organization. There were no counter-attacks. The men were keen; and though the left of the division was held up and machine-guns rattled out from a redoubt at least 1000 yards in the rear, the order was issued to advance to the storming of the village.

Once again at six o'clock in the cold and dark of the hour before dawn "we up-ped and at -ted 'em." The fight was not a day old before legends began to crystallize round the deeds of the leader. They were told in the trenches, in billets, and in the messes of the great. It was roundly asserted that he went on a hundred and fifty yards in front of the regiment and then stopped with a start. "Dear me," he said, "I believe I forgot to tell the men to follow me." But there is no need to call in rumour to stuff out the true myth of this adventure. The cold, simple, historical truth is that Beaucourt was stormed, taken by storm, occupied throughout its length and breadth in rather less than twenty minutes.

Just at first here and there a German post held, and a trench garrison faced the bomb and the bayonet. But no part of the onset was arrested. The gallant colonel and his men went across the village in manoeuvre

191

form and made good an almost semicircular trench round the far side of their precious jewel.

They could now count their gains and losses, lick their wounds, and reckon the victory. The colonel had received his fourth wound, and the ranks were smaller, though not a great deal smaller. The assault had been too quick and complete to be costly. The most obvious and least manageable booty was the concourse of prisoners. Though some enemy were seen bolting, the majority surrendered and were hurried back before they could be seen clearly enough to tempt their own guns. Beaucourt was another Courcellette, captured just as quickly and as an appendix, an afterthought, to the first victory.

The colonel stands out as clear a figure of the true fighting man as the Guardsman, Colonel John Vaughan Campbell, who blew his silver huntinghorn to the rally over the trenches by Lesbœufs - "Dauntless the slug-horn to his lips he set." If on this occasion the instrument was no more than a whistle it blew a note as silver as any "on Fontarabian echoes borne" in the times of Charlemagne romance.

On the left of the Naval Division fought a number of Scottish regiments who won laurels as green as any in their annals; and that is to say much. They were given the hardest task on the front; and their capture of Beaumont-Hamel and Y-ravine yields to no event in the war. Both were taken by storm within twelve hours - between 6 A.M. and 6 P.M. on 13th November - though they were super-fortresses, defended by large garrisons as heavily armed and munitioned as the men wished, and connected by tunnels with reserve depots of supplies and reinforcements.

Y-ravine is a serpent nearly half a mile long. The mouth of the serpent is wide open, its lips almost reaching the old front line of German trenches guarding the approach to Beaumont-Hamel. When the storming party advanced through the fog and reached the first German trench there poured from the mouth such a rush of flame that even these Scotsmen, where they directly fronted the blast, were forced to pause. The attack stopped dead at this point, but at this point only, and by a bold dash up to the very skirts of their own bursting shells, the troops just south of the ravine rushed one trench after another. At an early hour in the morning they had reached a point level with Beaumont-Hamel itself, and hammered blows on the body of the monster.

North of the ravine the fighting was yet harder and progress rather slower. But north and south the troops, not content with reaching their own special goal, attacked the flanks of the ravine along which they advanced. At 10 A.M. a platoon or so of men had forced a way into the stem of the letter Y, below the open mouth. All this part of the chasm is a terrible place to attack. It is made for defence. At the worst the sides are 30 feet deep, as straight as a cliff, as carious and treacherous as a slag heap. Dugouts are cut into the cliff, some capacious enough to hold almost a battalion, and so roofed as to defy artillery.

From the upper jaw of the gape a tunnel leads away back to the third line. The men who swarmed down the sides into the stem of the Y - or body of the snake - found themselves sandwiched. A large force, continually reinforced via the tunnel, held the jaw, and other enemy, also in touch with reinforcements, held the tail. These Scotsmen had won their way to the neighbourhood of this enviable position between an enemy's pincers by hard individual fighting organized spontaneously on the field. "It was a soldiers' battle," said a general, not without pride. He preferred that the credit should go rather to the men than the staff.

Every man helped his neighbour; and soon the fruits of such soldiership were gathered. Between twelve and one midday the Germans, finding themselves bombed on both sides, surrendered - just over 300 filed out in one group.

Incidents in the capture of prisoners were legion. A young officer, who had pushed through to a very distant point far in front of the rest, lost all his men but two, and they were sent off to guard approaches. He himself walked to the door of a battalion headquarters and told the German staff that they were his prisoners. They accepted his assertion, but, discovering his loneliness, lured him into an inner room and politely suggested that the position was reversed. He was the prisoner and they the captors. The interpretation was as politely accepted.

Now this inner room was fitted with a giant periscope, and the face of the German who was revolving it soon began to grow longer and longer. "British soldiers are all round us," he said at last, and at the word the Scots lieutenant quietly proposed to the room that the original position should be restored. "As you were." The first assertion, after all, was the right one. *They* were *his* prisoners. Throughout the incident and after it the German in command bore himself with a certain dignity and courtesy. His captive-captor said of him that "he behaved as a gentleman."

Good work, even in the capture of prisoners, was done by the signallers, many of whom went forward with the first wave. One of them found himself all alone and wounded at the mouth of a crowded German dugout. By way of occupation he told the men they were his prisoners, and then, using the telephone strapped round his body, called for assistance and guides for the prisoners.

The whole battle - this soldiers' battle - was marked by unnumbered episodes of individual personal acts of dash and coolness. Some men were too cool. They stopped to light German cigars, to taste the excellent food or don the enemy's helmets - which they wore hilariously for the rest of the day. One man, who discovered an ordnance store, deliberately changed his damp and muddy shirt for a clean German garment from the packets.

Our artillery was much more intense and more accurate than on 1st July, though here and there little bits of wire were undestroyed. Everywhere in the near neighbourhood of a trench the ground was like a Gruyere cheese. Beaumont-Hamel itself was pounded to the highest pitch of powerful precision, and the loss of observation on the day of battle made little difference to the accuracy of the final barrage.

Some of the nests, apart from their human occupants, were worth robbing. One food dump contained excellent butter, white bread, tinned hams, soda-water, and other luxuries. Cigars were "frequent and free," and the ordnance stores seem to have been of good quality. One brigade took 54 machine-guns and I heavy mortar.

I have left the rest of the battle 1000 yards and more in the rear. The right wing of the advance had been screened, as by a spur of the rise; but the left and centre were fully exposed to the ministrations of a redoubt peculiarly powerful and well placed, the same redoubt possibly that had caused the bitterest losses on 1st July. The redoubt just swells above the earth and wire like the back of a whale out of the water. It is roofed with reinforced concrete. Below it is capacious and well equipped with stores and the mechanism of defence. It has three chief exits, to which ladders lead. Dovetailed into the slope of the hill, its emplacements can rake the whole face of the country west and north; and nothing could live in its planes of fire. You would have said that no troops could pass it; but after continuous efforts on all sides various groups forced their way past, and irregular lines were won and made firm some distance beyond, while this monster was still nursed in the bosom of our position. Runners took back messages of a "nest" or "pocket" left uncleared. It was much more than that. It was a fortress, unharmed and not quite invested.

But it was not impregnable. Monster was to meet monster. Towards seven in the evening an inconspicuous carapace, a great sluggish, grunting beetle, was seen by the German garrison wriggling very slowly forward in arcs and at tangents, carefully avoiding any wounded who lay in its path. As if the scent was not good, though just sufficient, it nosed slowly forward, along and over the old German front trench. Earlier, an infantry officer was observed urging it on, like a master talking to an undecided bloodhound.

After many minutes it approached so near its crouching prey that it could surrender scent for sight. It prepared for action. What this dragon of the slime did, what flames came from its mouth, what threats were roared, I must not say in precise detail. But it did and threatened enough. Out of one of the mouths of the earth and concrete fortress appeared a white cloth waved on a stick. Not so much as a hand or arm was visible, but the flag of surrender waved. Firing ceased and the beast bellowed no more, but allowed its myrmidons to go forward and accept the surrender. Presently, crouching there, it watched nearly twenty score Germans file out, draw up in rank, and march back across the old front line. Good beast, it had done its part. Not what the infantry had done, but good service - good service.

Of the thousand and one episodes of this sphere of battle, none is more unofficial, more English, than the collecting of prisoners by a member of the force who had accompanied the rest as a supernumerary. After having gathered in several groups, he found the work becoming too extensive for his individual energies, so he formed a little limited company from his friends and together they developed the business rapidly. They were even accused of stealing 400 prisoners from the next division!

In regard to the prisoners the German wireless account brought out one charming point. It reported the appearance of British cavalry behind the infantry and conjectured that they were waiting to break through. The truth is that they were isolated groups preparing to act as escort to prospective prisoners; and they did not prove too numerous for the job. A number of the horses were in a lather and had done pretty well all they were capable of before noon.

Below the Ancre the attack moving down from the highlands as well as along the river was easier and not less complete. Perhaps no engagement in the war gained us more solid advantage at less cost. We had excellent observation for the previous preparations, so that the artillery crumpled up the river road, continually shrapnelled the culverts and bridges across the stream, and finally blew into the air the machine-gun emplacements and caches. When our men went over the parapet and forward to the attack, in the muggy obscurity of this autumn morning, neither they nor the enemy could see anything.

And the enemy was not altogether alert. His infantry, his machine-gunners, and in some measure his artillery were caught napping, or if ready, not ready to fight. At the moment the 223rd Division was relieving the 30th, which had been fifteen days in the trenches, so that the German garrison was for the moment very much bigger than usual, and perhaps for that reason less watchful. Our bombs, which we used in great quantity, fell into crowded trenches. Hundreds of the enemy's wounded, whom I afterwards met smiling contentedly in our hospitals or munching biscuits in our clearing stations, had bomb and grenade wounds, such wounds as the rest did not mean to have. Few waited for the bayonet. Hands went up as freely as the oars at a regatta salute, and 1300 soldiers with 29 officers were counted in the collecting station reserved for this single part of the attack before the fight was many hours old.

You would have said that the enemy had made themselves ready for their approaching migration. Many of the soldiers wore their coats, and a good number took from their pockets large stores of cigarettes. The officers carried complete packs; and some were a little insolent, because better rooms had not been provided them for the unpacking of their goods. It was explained to them that it is wiser on going to a new hotel among a foreign people to write or wire the news of your arrival.

The men evinced a very different temper from the officers. Following the general rule among prisoners, they at once began asking questions about the probable duration of the war. One of them, whose opinion seemed to be popular, said that anyway the war was over for Germany and he meant to set about liking England again as quickly as possible.

Even more remarkable than the attack was the sequel. Immediately after the trenches down to the river had been captured our men strolled about above ground as if they were out for an airing. They picked up relics. They shared out German cigars and sat on parapets smoking, and enjoyed to the hilt, for the little while that it lasted, the serenity of the battle-field. All the while the fight was raging furiously across the river; but the rush of the naval men had carried the battle almost beyond the line of the troops on the south.

The battle of the Somme was virtually over. During the next few days we shoved forward on the south of the Ancre and rounded off our victories on the north, taking more prisoners. But a week later we had settled down to winter quarters. The fullest page in British history was turned.

The sense of winter was over all armies. On the last day of November, the end of the fifth month of fighting that had cost the Germans and the French and ourselves nearly a million and a half of casualties, I wrote with the emotion of finality strong on the senses:

"The murk that has settled down over the country has added the last touch of brutality to battle-fields always incredibly brutal. Perhaps the silence helps. Few and fewer shells whine through the fog, and more and more of the few thump into the mud without explosion. All the firing is blind; and perhaps for that reason each shell fuller of fear; for the finer courage is debased into fatalism and mere reliance on the law of average. And in the mud and mist you notice the details of the battle-field in more particular detail, now that the general view is cut off and all ground is dead ground.

"The great crater by Beaumont-Hamel looks like the bed of an emptied lake strewn with the bodies and bits of the bodies of its old denizens. Here we blew up a quantity of German dugouts tunnelled into the side of the older crater; and the successive tons of explosive, besides doing their deadly work, have altered the very landscape. Close by, at the bottom of a trench, the Germans lie head to heel strung out in a line where they rushed from the escape mouth of their dugout into a cascade of bombs and perhaps an enfilading rifle. Egg-bombs and oyster-bombs and hairbrush bombs are scattered everywhere - small refuse left, it might be, by a receding tide, along with the burden of mud-drowned bodies.

"Day after day and night after night our burial parties have been at work. At any moment you may meet the padre returning with his group of men from the latest field burial. The business is nearly done, but it never quite ends. The Germans lived in this quarter for two years, working all the time, and left more caves than could be reckoned in a day, even if the shells had not rootled in the trough of mud and rubbish for five months. Stores and tombs still lie undiscovered, and diggers a century hence will still find discs and chains that were to announce the identity of the victims.

"The power of ugliness could no further go. Everything visible or audible or tangible to the senses - to touch, smell, and perception - is ugly beyond imagination. The hanks of wrenched and rotted wire suggest that the very soil has turned into a sort of matter hostile to all kindly productiveness. And so will the waste look till spring comes and proves that after all fertility lives. Indeed, lest mere disgust and despair should be bred by the spectacle of ruin, nature is already sending a message of spring, a miracle of the season.

"The miracle is this: that the battered trees, just now as bare as telegraph poles, are putting out young, green leaves; and in one place great comfrey leaves even now conceal the very whereabouts of a trench we pounded and captured during this battle of the Somme."

CHAPTER XVI
EPILOGUE

THE BATTLE OF the Somme was over, and all the world had leisure to review it and interpret its meaning. The cannons bellowed still. The stream of men went down to the sea and flowed back with the tide. The aeroplanes hummed overhead. Generals met in conference. Intelligence officers gathered news of the enemy. Deserters, if not prisoners, slowly filtered back. Engineers were if possible busier than ever.

But everywhere you knew that battle, real battle, was over till such time as the soaked ground should give up its excess of moisture to the attraction of longer sunlight. Leave was longer. Tired nurses took medical leave in the South of France, and throughout the hospitals, doctors, though busy with such maladies as trench feet, could take a full night's rest and have time to review their work. At last all of us began to have time to ask the meaning of what we had seen and felt during five months of life too quick and changeful for any perspective.

While the battle raged the mechanism of battle, the murder of the battle-field, the drama of particular deeds, corporate and individual, filled the mind. A great gun I often visited shot so hard that the whole of its weighty platform, sunk into the solid ground, retreated by the whole width of its base. I could see the many hundredweight of its shell careering like a ghostly curse German-wards, and the force of the recoil, pushing back the solid earth, stood to me for symbol of the mass of buttress the building of such a battle demanded. It needed the bulk of a nation to push forward such a monster and hold it there. Guns and aeroplanes and balloons and bombs and gas cylinders were forced on the mind's eye as clearly as that strange chain dragged by Marley's ghost before the frightened eyes of Scrooge.

The battle-field was as impressive, as insistent. Week after week the miles of murdered countryside - dismantled woods, dis housed villages, disembowelled fields - were burnt into the vision. Silhouettes of upright fragments - a bit of gaping roof leaning against a tumbling wall in Mametz; a twisted stanchion bridging the hole of an uprooted tree in Maurepas, the Tank crossing a trench in Thièpval - such desolate pictures uprose before the sleeping and waking mind.

Everyday tales of derring do were told. So many were these, so strange, so Olympian, that you lost the men in the drama, and pursuing the plot forgot the character. An airman hit with the wing of his plane the wire holding a balloon, and the wire penetrated the wing and held firm against the rib. The pace of the machine, the slant of the wire, the strength of the hold sent the plane circling round and round its tie, and at the same time sliding to the ground, where at last it landed safe. What chance has psychology or thought of tendencies, or even sentiment and emotion, against stirring tales of this sort!

At last the mind was released by winter rest and stirred to other thoughts by the entry of a new year. At once it swung back to things more essential than machines or pictures or events, and could see that the crowning marvel of the Somme was man. The British Army may have made many score of mistakes. Commanders ordered men to attack unbroken wire, gunners fired at their own trenches, engineers miscalculated dump areas, infantry fired at one another in the woods or lost their way foolishly or left the burden to their neighbours but were the mistakes in tactics multiplied indefinitely it would still remain that the crowning wonder and triumph of the battle of the Somme was the British Army itself.

The battle was opened by troops from the British Isles and one battalion from our oldest colony; but before its end all the Empire had taken part. The South Africans fought a seven days' deadly struggle in Delville Wood. The Australians took Pozières and fought a yet tougher battle against the mud near Warlencourt. The New Zealanders did their own work and much of their neighbours to the west of Gueudecourt, always winning and minimising casualties by virtue of mere pluck and quickness. The Canadians took over from the Australians and later captured trenches and villages with the impetus of French troops at their best. Even some few Indians were engaged in that small and dashing cavalry adventure south of High Wood. The Irish along the Ancre and at Ginchy, the Welsh at Mametz, and the Scotch everywhere and always proved their best racial qualities. From Mametz on 1st July to Beaumont-Hamel on 13th November we won trenches, villages, woods, redoubts by virtue of the native virtues of grit, self-reliance, obstinacy, and good sense.

If one were to examine the public, the readers of newspapers and war books on the achievements of the war, they would all have in their memory some fine deed by the Irish, the Scotch, the Australians, the Canadians, and the rest. How many would quote you the achievement of any purely English unit?

But no record of the battle, of the war, is true that does not give credit to the English for native virtues as potent and constant and distinct as any district in the world possesses. English troops have been the cement of the battle. "Thank God for the Staffordshire miners." "By happy fortune we followed some good old county troops who had done their trenches properly." "These English troops always 'stick it.'" Such little phrases I have heard day after day through the long warfare. And when you are among troops from overseas or any local regiment you find among them a thickening of pure Englishmen, especially among the corporals - the place a man reaches because he is to be trusted, not because he is clever or pushful or big.

Doubtless one county differs from another, and a great gulf is fixed between the townsman and the countryman, between the Cockney and the Wilts labourer. But they claim a common quality of taking things as they come, they doing their job without advertisement, without self-congratulation, and often with a very pretty turn of quiet humour. The Cockneys in High Wood, the Bedfords at the Quadrilateral, the War wicks, Gloucesters, Wilts, Sussex, Surrey, Kents and the rest round Thièpval, went through the fight and came out of it without loss of fibre or increase of pride.

Those of us who spoke to these troops almost daily as they came out or went into action felt this English quality as it cannot be felt outside the area of battle. The highest thrills I associate with Australians, Canadians, and Scotch. Their deeds and emotions remain the most salient in the memory, and yet the battle in retrospect is essentially English. One has the impression that the English gave the others their chance to shine, as a pack of good, indistinguishable forwards give the openings to the half and three quarter-backs, whose names and features are known to every other spectator.

You observe this quality more perhaps in billets than in the trench. Indeed, sometimes even the sight of a battle, of infantry advancing in the open, and great shells bursting in front of you, and indeed at intervals around you, is less moving than the subsequent tale of the fight as told by Englishmen who have just come out.

Very tired, very modest, and very glad of rest, they tumble into their billets; and there, in barns or houses or huts or tents, they bless their stars for a few quiet days; and under pressure will confess that the fight was "a bit stiff, though nothing exceptional" They might be at home in peace-time. Then slowly they begin to recall and discuss incidents which for the first time do seem even to themselves a little remarkable.

The best of the English soldier is that he never feels himself a hero. You would have thought that the old county troops who took hill trenches and beat the Prussian Guard on the Thièpval slope would have been conscious of some exultation; but most of them chiefly felt pride, I think, in the individual feats of others. One of these (from that desperate artillery fighting south of Thièpval on 26th July) was one of the very strangest in the war. It is the tale of a runner. There is no one more calmly persistent in doing his job than these English runners. On this night one of them was sent back from our newly taken trench with an important message at a time when the German bombardment was peculiarly fast and furious. The Wilts and Worcesters, from whose ranks he came, were being pounded with all the weight of metal that the enemy could command; and his artillery has never been stronger.

The runner passed through unscathed, and presently returned with an answer. He had twice passed through the curtain of howitzer fire.

Indeed, the shells had fallen in such profusion during his absence that the landscape was quite changed. The trenches that had been signposts were battered to the state of confusing pits and paths.

The runner thought his journey was unduly prolonged, but he went on - that was his business - and in reward presently came to a trench. Being cautious as well as courageous, he looked in before leaping, and saw, not good, kind Englishmen, but crouching Prussians packed tight beneath a frieze of bayonets. The sight was enough to sate his curiosity, and he retired again in safety. His experience was instantly reported to the artillery, and immediately our heavy shells followed the example of the runner and also looked into the Prussian trench.

It was the very moment when the Guard - the 28th Regiment of the Prussian Fusiliers - had decided to charge. One wave came over the parapet, and as it came was broken here, there, and everywhere. Its last ripple faded into flatness 50 yards from the trench. A second followed. The last surviving unit of it may have travelled 60 yards. No more made the venture. The attack was broken. Since they caught the Prussians north-east of Contalmaison our heavies never did more thorough work.

But the hardship of the battle, the thing that won the battle, as the General said, was the extreme serenity of the troops under a murderous bombardment. They were as calm and efficient when it was over as when it began. They were weaker only by the sum of the actual losses.

Always the men keep heroism at arm's length. A little tough shireman who had done great work in a German trench described to me how he had met a German "big enough to eat me for breakfast and not feel hungry after" Did he go on to describe how he David killed this Goliath? Not at all. He said he was "fair scared, but didn't like to run away." And while he was not liking to run away the great German put up his hands.

Nearly all men, perhaps the English more than the rest, hate fighting. Among the press of wounded men coming back from battle you will find the Englishman as a rule plodding on contentedly and thinking of his chance of going home, while the others are still full of the battle. Especially do I remember walking and talking with a stream of men coming back from a great fight in July near Montauban. Scotch, Irish, and English soldiers all swept across a very wide interval between trenches in more than international form; the wounded, even the twice-wounded, went forward with the hale, and met the enemy waiting for them at the first goal-line. Some of the quickest work was done by South English troops; but almost all were inarticulate. Many of the others said memorable things and evinced a real joy in hand-to-hand fighting. "It makes it a bit cheerier to have a go with the bayonet," said a twice-wounded Scotsman, forced at last to sit on his haunches and lick his wounds before hobbling back through the shells. He used this amazing word "cheerier" without the least suspicion of humour.

Another man from overseas who was on his way back with a bullet in the forearm and a shell wound in the calf said: "One doesn't want to come so far and not have a go at 'em with the steel." "So far" means a voluntary journey of, I suppose, some 12,000 miles. And he added the finest compliment that any nation could desire, of a sort that no other nation perhaps has ever received: "It will be fine, too, to go home. *I've never been there.*"

Let Germans who trust to the fostering of seditions in the Antipodes and elsewhere study that idiom of "home." It will penetrate as deep as did the bayonet of the man who had "never been there" but fought for it with a fire beyond the reach of the greencoats - tough fighters though they are - who knelt on the trench's lip before him crying, "Mercy, kamerad, mercy!"

The parts of the Empire that are not England have contributed to the common stock zeal and talent and devotion that have woven the stuff of victory. No one who thinks imperially desires distinctions; but we may recognize that the readiness of the English to acknowledge and indeed proclaim the virtues of all the rest has been the master cause of the welding of this varied army into a united force moving with one will and intention. Home is home, and is called home because of a sort of magnanimous modesty in the English people. And that is why the refrain of the Hymn of Hate is: ENGLAND.

5	6	7	8	9	10
15	16	17	18	19	20
25	26	27	28	29	30
35	36	37	38	39	
45	46	47	48	49	
		57	58		